MOMENTUM

IGNITE
YOUR
LIFE
IN 25 DAYS

LANCE WITT

true spirituality™

Published in Suwanee, Georgia, by Living on the Edge

Unless otherwise noted, Scripture quotations are taken from the Holy Bible, New International Version°, Copyright © 1973, 1978, 1984 by Biblica, Inc.™ Used by permission of Zondervan. All rights reserved worldwide. www.zondervan.com.

Scriptures marked updated NIV are taken from The Holy Bible, updated New International Version°. Copyright © 1973, 1978, 1984, 2011 by Biblica, Inc.™ Used by permission of Zondervan. All rights reserved worldwide. www.zondervan.com.

Scriptures marked NLT are taken from *The Holy Bible*, New Living Translation. © 1996, 2004, 2007 by Tyndale House Foundation. Used by permission of Tyndale House Publishers, Inc., Carol Stream, Illinois 60188. All rights reserved.

Scriptures marked NASB are taken from the NEW AMERICAN STANDARD BIBLE°, © 1960, 1962, 1963, 1968, 1971, 1972, 1973, 1975, 1977, 1995 by The Lockman Foundation. Used by permission.

Library of Congress Cataloging-in-Publication Data
ISBN 978-1-60593-169-2
Printed in the United States of America

Edited by Philis Boultinghouse
Design by Stephanie D. Walker; www.water2winedesign.com

This book is dedicated to two couples
who have a combined investment in my life
of more than eighty years. I am speaking of...

Glen and Margaret Witt (my parents)
And
Joe and Betty Chandler (my in-laws)

I have more than fifty years of relationship with my parents
and over thirty with my in-laws.

To all four of you, I want to say thanks for ...
Loving Jesus
Serving His bride
Believing in me
Modeling a great marriage
Living your faith

I will always be profoundly grateful.

CONTENTS

FOREWORD

I love basketball, playing it and watching it. In almost every professional basketball game, there is a shift that has everything to do with the title of this book. It is a *momentum* shift. The scenario goes something like this… the visiting team is ahead by a few points, but the home team scores a couple of quick baskets. Then they steal the ball and score an easy dunk. The home crowd erupts in applause. The momentum has clearly shifted, and everyone knows it. At this moment, something predictable happens. The visiting coach calls a time out. Why? Because momentum has been lost, and the team needs time to regroup and make the necessary adjustments.

Far worse than losing momentum on the basketball court is losing momentum spiritually. I've been in ministry a long time, and I've listened to the stories of thousands of people. A theme I've heard over and over again is that people feel stuck spiritually…they have lost momentum. Sometimes it is just the grind of life that causes us to get stuck. Sometimes it is poor judgment and bad choices. And sometimes it is just a slow drift that results in spiritual lethargy and that missing sense of "God's presence."

In my recent book *Living on the Edge,* I was like that coach calling a time out—providing time to regroup and make some adjustments so that *Christians can start living like Christians.* From Romans 12, I provided an actual profile of a disciple and a proven pathway that will create spiritual momentum!

A Romans 12 disciple is someone who is…

- Surrendered to God
- Separate from the world's values
- Sober in self-assessment
- Serving in love
- Supernaturally responding to evil with good

The apostle Paul has given us clear teaching and principles for being disciples. But sometimes we need more than the message; we need a model. We not only need life principles, we need living pictures. We not only need truth, we need testimonies from real people who can show us how to live.

That's exactly what my good friend Lance Witt has done in this twenty-five-day devotional. He has taken each of these principles from Romans 12 and has shown us what they look like in the life of an Old Testament character. Lance has also provided clear and concrete ways to put these principles into action in your everyday life.

His engaging style will bring these Old Testament characters to life. He will give you fresh insight into the life and journey of some of the great heroes of our faith. These men are the all star players from the past. But Lance doesn't allow us to put these heroes on a pedestal. He helps us to see that they were ordinary people who lived extraordinary lives. Sometimes they got stuck and lost momentum.

But they lived well and followed God wholeheartedly.

As you walk with these great trailblazers of the faith over the next twenty-five days, may you be inspired, challenged, and encouraged. And may you feel the *momentum* begin to build.

Chip Ingram
Author, *Living on the Edge; Dare to Experience True Spirituality*
Senior Pastor, Venture Christian Church

introduction

ORDINARY PEOPLE LIVING EXTRAORDINARY LIVES

Whenever we pick up the Bible and read the stories, we are tempted to make the biblical characters larger than life. We tend to think they were superhuman—that they never had a bad day, never fought with their spouses, never yelled at their kids, and never got ticked off when another camel cut them off in traffic. Nothing could be further from the truth. They were just like us. Ordinary. Common. Flawed. Pudgy. Unrefined. Bald. Normal.

And they weren't perfect. They had a sin nature just like you and me. At times they lost momentum and got spiritually stuck just like us. One of the great things about the Bible is that it doesn't airbrush its characters. We are allowed to see their great faith and their great failures. We get a front-row seat to their real-life battles with anger and temptation and relationships and money and . . . faith.

In this devotional we will look at five of those Old Testament characters. We are going to spend time with Abraham, Daniel, Moses, Jonathan, and Joseph. It's my prayer that your interaction with them in these pages will not be as mystical supersaints, but rather as ordinary people who teach us how to live in the trenches of everyday life.

The premise of this devotional comes from Chip Ingram and his book *Living on the Edge.*[1] In his book, Chip gives us a profile of a disciple from Romans 12. I'm grateful for his insightful writing, and I have used some of his thoughts in this devotional book.

In Romans 12, Paul gives us the *teaching*, and the Old Testament characters we'll be looking at give us the *testimony*. Paul gives us the *principles*, and these men give us the *practices*. Paul gives us the *concept* of a disciple, and these men give us the *conduct* of a disciple.

- Abraham models a life of surrender.
- Daniel exemplifies what it means to live separate from the world's values.
- Moses is a classic case study in having a sober self-assessment.
- Jonathan fleshes out what it looks like to serve others in love.
- And Joseph is the poster child of supernaturally responding to evil with good.

As you read and reflect on these pages, may God ignite your life and give you the courage to believe that ordinary people really can live extraordinary lives.

part 1

surrender

ABRAHAM

Therefore, I urge you, brothers,

in view of God's mercy,

to offer your bodies as living sacrifices,

holy and pleasing to God—

this is your spiritual act of worship.

—Romans 12:1

LOSING CAN MEAN WINNING

On April 6, 1865, over six thousand confederate soldiers were captured. The end was imminent. On the morning of April 9, General Robert E. Lee and his hungry men found themselves surrounded by five times as many Union soldiers as those who stood with him. Lee had no choice but to surrender.[1]

It would be impossible to describe the anguish of the troops when word went out that surrender was inevitable. When General Lee appeared after the surrender, a shout of welcome instinctively ran through the troops. But their shouts soon gave way to silence. Every hat was raised, and the soldiers' worn faces were bathed with tears.

As General Lee rode slowly along the lines, hundreds of his devoted veterans pressed around him. With tears flowing freely down his manly cheeks, the general said good-bye to his army.

Surrender. It's an ominous and intimidating word that can conjure up images of raising white flags and laying down arms. It can make us think of giving in and giving up. Defeat and humiliation often go hand in hand with surrender.

So when we talk about surrender being vital to the Christian life, it can sound hard and harsh, unless we are surrendering to something better. The apostle Paul talks about surrender (total commitment) in Romans 12:1 when he says, "Therefore, I urge you, brothers, in view of God's mercy, to offer your bodies as living sacrifices, holy and pleasing to God—this is your spiritual act of worship." Offering our bodies to God as a living sacrifice can seem daunting.

In ancient times, when animals were offered on the altar, the sacrifice was total and final. That is the imagery in Romans 12:1. Paul is calling on us to willingly crawl up on the altar and offer ourselves in total and final surrender. There is no such thing as partial surrender.

This call to offer our bodies as living sacrifices is bookended by two interesting phrases. First, Paul says that we offer ourselves "in view of God's mercy." Surrender is in response to God's mercy. When you really grasp what you were saved from, when you deep down feel the undeserved and free grace that liberated you, surrender is motivated by gratitude. Surrender is saying to God, "Because of all you've done for me and in me, everything I am and everything I have I gladly surrender to you."

Second, Paul says that our surrender is a "spiritual act of worship." The word translated "spiritual" in this verse means 'logical' or 'reasonable' or 'acceptable'. If God really is the king, ruler, and CEO of the universe, and if he really did send his son to die for me; then it is "logical" for me to surrender to him as an act of worship. God wants the same place in my life that he already has in the universe. And that is reasonable.

Our problem is that we tend to focus on what we are giving up rather than what we are getting in exchange. We fail to understand that "Total commitment [surrender] is the channel through which God's best and biggest blessings flow."[2] The Bible says that God wants you to experience abundant life—right here and right now. And the conduit through which God takes his blessings and pours them into your life is a pipe called *surrender.*

In the next few days, we'll be looking at the life and times of one man who surrendered all. Abraham not only offered his own life as a "living sacrifice"; he literally offered his only son. Abraham's life of faith was immortalized for our benefit so that we, too, can learn what true surrender is all about.

So what keeps us from surrender? Deep down, at the root of our fears is usually a misunderstanding of God and his character. If we are honest, many of us would have to say that we don't really believe that God is good and that he has our best interests at heart. We think God is holding out on us. And we question whether God really has the equation for the "good life."

Psalm 84:11 says, "For the LORD God is a sun and shield; the LORD gives grace and glory; no good thing does He withhold from those who walk uprightly" (NASB). Push rewind. Listen carefully to those words. God is a sun (provider) and shield (protector). He is all about grace and relationship. He is not about rules and performance. And "no good things does He withhold from those who walk uprightly." God's desire for you is more and better than you could ever imagine. When we walk surrendered to him, his promise to us is that he will pour out the abundant life.

> So when we talk about surrender being vital to the Christian life, it can sound hard and harsh, unless we are surrendering to something better.

That's just who he is. It is God's nature and character to pour good gifts on undeserving people.

Romans 8:32 says, "He who did not spare his own Son, but gave him up for us all, how will he not also, along with him, graciously give us all things?"

Because God is a good father and because we *trust* his heart, we can with confidence *entrust* our hearts to him.

It's like the difference between a white flag and a wedding. Both are symbols of surrender. The white flag of surrender is one of defeat and giving up. It represents what you lose. A wedding is a different kind of surrender. In a wedding you surrender your heart out of love and relationship. It is not at all about what you lose, but rather what you gain. God wants you to know that his challenge to surrender is about a wedding, not a white flag.

WHAT ABOUT YOU?

What are you afraid of when you think of surrendering to God? What are you hesitant to give up? As you remember the bookends of God's call to surrender—his mercy and the reasonableness of his invitation—you will be on your way to trusting him with *you.*

Today's Takeaway
Surrender is trusting God's heart
toward you and entrusting your heart to him.

day
2

GOD'S COSMIC GPS

She was nothing more than contestant 43,212 when Susan Boyle stepped on the stage of *Britain's Got Talent*. As a forty-seven-year-old church volunteer, it was a big step to sing on national television. Little did she know how that one performance would forever change the trajectory of her life. Within nine days of the audition, videos of Boyle had been viewed over 100 million times.[1]

You're never too old to start a new adventure.

At age seventy-five, a man named Abraham took a big step and began a new adventure. At seventy-five, most people are looking for security and comfort, not risk and adventure. At seventy-five, most people are looking to move closer to family, not farther away. At seventy-five, most people are finishing, not starting.

But when you are truly surrendered you don't always do what most people do. Living the "good life" as defined by society is very different than living the "God life." Surrender and adventure tend to go together . . . no matter your age.

At age seventy-five, God invites Abraham into an adventure. This unexpected invitation would require him to leave behind all that was familiar and start over.

Ur was home for Abraham and Sarah. They had grown up there. They had married there. Their family was there. They had made their livelihood there. They had friends there. Their roots went deep in the land of Ur. It was all they had known. But God was about to change all of that.

Hebrews 11:8 says, "By faith Abraham, when he was called, obeyed by going out to a place which he was to receive for an inheritance; and he went out, not knowing where he was going" (NASB).

What was clear to Abraham was the call from God and the promise of an inheritance. What was unclear was where he was going or how he was going to get there.

God has a long history of asking people to step out in faith without fully knowing where they are going. In fact, it seems rare that God ever lays out the whole plan at the beginning.

God tends to operate like a cosmic GPS. Think about the GPS (global positioning system) you might have in your car. The GPS doesn't give you all the directions at once. It gives you just enough instructions to get started and then it reveals each set of directions as you need them. It is like that woman's voice inside the little box is saying, "Trust me. I know the destination and the steps it will take to get there. So sit back, relax, and enjoy the ride."

In the same way, God says to Abraham: "Trust me. I know the destination, and I will lead you step by step." Abraham's response to God is recorded in Genesis 12. These nine words aren't preceded by any fanfare or hype, but they were a defining moment in Abraham's life: "So Abram left, as the LORD had told him" (Genesis 12:4). Those nine words reflect faith followed by obedience.

So how could Abraham pack up his stuff, load up his family, and head to an unknown destination? Hebrews 11:6 provides us with a clue to the answer: "Without faith it is impossible to please Him, for he who comes to God must believe that He is and that He is a rewarder of those who seek Him" (NASB). At the heart of Abraham's faith was a fundamental belief that God is real and that he is good. Notice those words: "He is a rewarder of those who seek Him."

> God has a long history of asking people to step out in faith without fully knowing where they are going.

In Matthew 7:11 Jesus helps us see the benevolent character of God. "So if you sinful people know how to give good gifts to your children, how much more will your heavenly Father give good gifts to those who ask him" (NLT).

Behind Abraham's obedience and radical step of faith was knowledge that God is a good father. What gives you confidence to step out in faith is a settled conviction that God is kind and gracious.

WHAT ABOUT YOU?

Has God been prompting you to leave what's comfortable and follow him into the unknown? Is he inviting you into a faith adventure? Just remember that little voice coming out of the GPS: "Trust me. I know the destination and the steps it will take to get there. So sit back, relax, and enjoy the ride."

Today's Takeaway
Your confidence in the God you know is what gives you confidence to step into the unknown.

⊙12

SURRENDERED PEOPLE HAVE NO RIGHTS

In 2002, on a cold November day, Leigh Anne Touhy was driving down the street, minding her own business. By God's providence she saw something that was unusual in her part of town. What she saw was someone named Michael Oher. The intersection of their lives that night would forever change both of them. He was a young, homeless African-American teenager. With a drug-addicted mom and a dad he'd never met, sixteen-year old Michael Oher was struggling to stay in school. He had a 0.6 grade point average.

Leigh Anne invited Michael to spend the night out of the rain in their affluent, suburban West Memphis home. The Touhys ended up inviting Michael to live with them and made him part of their family. They helped him improve his grades, graduate from high school, and earn a scholarship to play college football. Ultimately, Michael was drafted into the National Football League. His story was eventually told in the movie *The Blind Side.* And it was all possible because one wealthy, suburban Christian woman who was surrendered to God chose to be unselfish. You see, surrendered people are unselfish people.[1]

Thousands of years earlier we find an example of this kind of unselfishness in Abraham's life. His financial portfolio was also impressive. His investments in agribusiness and precious metals had paid huge returns. Genesis 13:2 provides a snapshot of Abraham's personal financial statement. He "had become very wealthy in livestock and in silver and gold." But God had also blessed Abraham's nephew Lot, and with increased prosperity came increased challenges and tension. The Bible says the land couldn't support both of them, and friction between the two family businesses erupted.

Truly surrendered followers of Jesus don't have a spirit of entitlement. ...It's not all about you.

So Abraham stepped forward and offered a surprising solution to the problem. In order to preserve peace in the family, Abraham unselfishly offered Lot the option of choosing whichever land he desired and Abraham took whatever was left over. Abraham, as the oldest leader of the family, had every right to claim the best land. Yet Abraham deferred. He was generous and unselfish.

Whether it is Leigh Anne Tuohy in modern-day Memphis or Abraham in ancient Negev, when we discover surrender, unselfishness is not far behind.

Truly surrendered followers of Jesus put people ahead of possessions. Abraham cared more about his family than he did getting the most desirable land. He put relationship ahead of real estate.

When you are surrendered, you hold the things of this world loosely because . . .

- You realize that this world is not your home.
- Your life isn't defined by possessions.
- You don't really own anything. Everything you have is simply on loan from God. You are a manager, not an owner.
- You trust that God will take care of you.

There is tremendous freedom in being surrendered. It takes the pressure off. Knowing that God will take care of you, you can focus on people.

In Philippians 2:3–4, Paul challenges us, "Do nothing out of selfish ambition or vain conceit, but in humility consider others better than yourselves. Each of you should look not only to your own interests, but also to the interests of others."

Truly surrendered followers of Jesus don't have a spirit of entitlement. We hate to see entitlement in others, and it's unbecoming in any Christ-follower. When you have surrendered to Jesus as King of your life and have died to self, you don't have to grab for your rights. When you are surrendered, you know that it's not all about you and that waiving your rights is the way of surrender.

Jesus beautifully modeled this for us. Like Abraham, Jesus could have asserted his rights, but in surrender to his Father he laid aside his "rightful" place in heaven and went to the cross.

The apostle Paul encourages us to follow Jesus' example of surrender. "Your attitude should be the same as that of Christ Jesus: Who, being in very nature God, did not consider equality with God something to be grasped, but made himself nothing, taking the very nature of a servant, being made in human likeness" (Philippians 2:5–7).

Today, work hard at waiving your rights and unselfishly serving others.

WHAT ABOUT YOU?

How are you doing in the "putting people ahead of possessions" department? Or the "holding the things of this world loosely" part? As you do, you'll discover the amazing freedom that comes from surrender.

Today's Takeaway

Surrender and unselfishness go hand in hand.

◉12

day
4

DON'T JUST DO SOMETHING
. . . SIT THERE!

I had a lot going on that day, but I was right on time for my doctor's appointment. I swiftly walked through the doors and approached the counter. I stood there for a couple of minutes before someone came to help me. I was instructed to sign in, and then I heard those ominous words: "Take a seat in the waiting room." I sat down, hopeful that my time of confinement in the waiting room would be brief. I quickly rifled through the out-of-date magazines. I checked the news on my iPhone. I texted my wife. I read my latest e-mails. And that was in the first three minutes. I might have been in "idle" on the outside, but my engine was racing on the inside.

And then the injustice came. Someone who came in after me got called before me. I couldn't believe it. There was no explanation, no apology, no refund. Just blatant unfairness. Did these people not know that I had important things to do? Did they not know that they were wasting my time?

As you can probably tell, I struggle just a little with waiting. But my suspicion is that you do too.

Whether it's the doctor's office, the DMV, the airport, or a grocery store line, when we have to wait, we usually end up restless and agitated. Waiting feels so unproductive and passive. For busy, driven, active people in the twenty-first century, waiting doesn't seem like a virtue; it seems like a waste of time.

But St. Augustine said, "Patience is the companion of wisdom." How many times have we made unwise decisions because we didn't have the patience to wait?

While in a season of waiting, impatience led Abraham and Sarah to make a very unwise decision. God had promised Abraham a child. But almost ten years had passed since the promise, and their biological clocks were ticking. Time was running out, and God wasn't doing anything. Have you ever felt like that? The chances of Sarah getting pregnant were growing slimmer by the day. She was tired of waiting. As waiting increased, trust in God decreased.

Then Sarah found a loophole in the promise of God. He had promised Abraham a child, but he hadn't said anything about Sarah being the mother. So she devised a plan to arrange for a surrogate mother. In essence, she came up with a strategy that involved using adultery to help fulfill God's promise.

Abraham agreed to the plan and slept with Sarah's handmaid, Hagar, and Hagar became pregnant and gave birth to Ishmael (Genesis 15–16). As you can imagine, this plan resulted in all kinds of dysfunction, bitterness, and chaos.

In God's own time, he did give Abraham and Sarah the son of promise. The conflict today between Israel and the Arab nations traces back to Ishmael and Isaac. The consequences of Abraham and Sarah's unwillingness to wait on God still reverberate through history even to this day.

Part of being surrendered to God is learning to wait. It is learning to trust him even when you can't see what he's doing. It's learning to be patient even when there are no answers coming from heaven. God's stopwatch doesn't run the same as ours. In 2 Peter 3:8 we read, "But you must not forget this one thing, dear friends: A day is like a thousand years to the Lord, and a thousand years is like a day" (NLT). God won't be rushed. He is not in a hurry.

When you're surrendered, you realize that God doesn't owe you anything. When you're surrendered, you begin to understand that God cares more about your character than your comfort. You learn that God's greatest desire for you is to be holy, not happy.

Often God uses waiting to forge character and holiness. So he makes us sit in the waiting room of life. He doesn't tell us when he is coming. He doesn't send an angel to update us. He doesn't explain his delay. He just says, *Wait.*

> God cares more about your character than your comfort.

If we don't learn to wait, we will be frustrated with God and will question his goodness. Or, like Abraham and Sarah, we will take matters in our own hands. Our circumstances might be screaming, "Don't just sit there . . . *do* something!" But God is whispering, *Don't just do something . . . sit there!*

WHAT ABOUT YOU?

Maybe you are in a season of waiting right now. Maybe you are facing a situation you can't control or fix. Or perhaps your spouse has left or you're facing a severe illness. Maybe you have lost a job or have a rebellious child. You desperately want God to do something, but all you hear is, *Wait . . . not yet.* When God's answer is wait, a question is imbedded in that answer: *Will you trust me?*

May your prayer be that of the psalmist in Psalm 130:5: "I wait for the LORD, my soul waits, and in his word I put my hope."

Today's Takeaway

"Patience is the companion of wisdom" (St. Augustine).

day 5

GOD'S THRONE
IS A SINGLE-SEATER

Imagine that one day my wife walks by my computer and sees a picture of another attractive woman on my screensaver. Let me tell you what her response will *not* be. She will not say, "Well, that's interesting, but my husband has a right to his privacy. His other relationships really aren't my business. Who am I to nag him about his personal life?"

No! With some passion and more than a little anger, she would demand some answers. Inherent in our marriage commitment is an expectation of undivided devotion.

In the same way, inherent in my faith commitment to Christ is an expectation of undivided devotion. God speaks of this expectation in Exodus 20 when he warns of idols: "You must not bow down to them or worship them, for I, the LORD your God, am a jealous God who will not tolerate your affections for any other gods!" (v. 5 NLT).

As Martin Luther pointed out, "Whatever your heart clings to and relies upon, that is your god."

When we place anything above God, that is actually *idolatry*—a term we don't use much today. At its core, idolatry is misplacing our affection, our devotion, and our love. It is putting something or someone else on the throne of our lives. One thing we know about a throne is that it is a single-seater, and God is not willing to share the throne of our lives with anyone or anything.

Along the journey of life, we pass through times when God tests our devotion to him. He will call on us to surrender, give up, or let go of anything that has begun to crowd his rightful place on the throne of our lives.

God is not willing to share the throne of our lives with anyone or anything.

In Genesis 22, God gave Abraham more than just a test. It is the mother of all tests. He didn't ask Abraham to surrender a job or a house or a hobby. He called on him to surrender his son Isaac. The son of promise. The son of his old age. The son who would carry on the family name.

Actually, the call was not just to surrender his son, but to sacrifice his son—to kill him. God was asking Abraham to literally, physically sacrifice Isaac as a burnt offering on top of Mount Moriah. Don't let your familiarity with the story lessen how horrifying this would be for a dad.

Amazingly, early the next morning, Abraham stepped out in obedience. And he did so rather matter-of-factly. The Bible says he loaded his donkey, cut some wood, conscripted two servants, and then he and Isaac headed off for a three-day journey to the mountains (Genesis 22:3).

Wouldn't it have been fascinating to overhear the conversation between Abraham and God during that journey? Each step was a test of deliberate obedience.

Then came the moment of truth. Abraham built an altar, tied up his son, and laid him on it. He then took the knife and raised it to slay his own son . . . when, finally, God stopped him at the last second. How could Abraham go that far? How could he be willing to kill his only son? We learn from the New Testament that Abraham actually believed God would raise Isaac from the dead (Hebrews 11:19). He had never seen or even heard of someone being raised from the dead. But Abraham so strongly believed in God's promise that blessings would come through Isaac that he trusted God to do the miraculous in order to keep his promise.

At the heart of Abraham's surrender was a belief in God's promises, God's character, and God's goodness.

At that moment, with knife in hand and his arm raised, Abraham was saying to God, "I'm all in. There is nothing I've held back from you."

Ponder this prayer from pastor and author A. W. Tozer: "Father, I want to know thee, but my cowardly heart fears to give up its toys. . . . I come trembling, but I do come. Please root from my heart all those things which I have cherished so long and which have become a part of my living self, so that Thou mayest enter and dwell there without a rival."[1]

WHAT ABOUT YOU?

What is sitting on your single-seater throne? Is it your kids? Your determination to get ahead? Your favorite hobby? What? Are you willing to allow God his rightful place on the throne of your life? Remember, surrender is the channel through which God's best and biggest blessings flow.

Today's Takeaway
There is no such thing as partial surrender.

ℚ12

living separate from the world's values

DANIEL

Do not conform any longer to the pattern of this world,

but be transformed by the renewing of your mind.

Then you will be able to test and approve what God's will is—

his good, pleasing and perfect will.

—Romans 12:2

FATHER KNOWS BEST

When I was a kid I loved to go to the state fair. One of my favorite attractions was the fun house. It had moving floors, zigzagging stairs, shifting walls, optical illusions, and an assortment of mirrors. But these were no ordinary mirrors. These mirrors had the ability to totally distort your shape and appearance.

For many Christians, their view of God comes from a kind of spiritual fun house mirror. It is distorted and inaccurate. Perhaps from what we learned at home or what we experienced at church, many of us grew up thinking of God as a cosmic drill sergeant. We envisioned him as mean-spirited, rules-focused, and virtually impossible to please.

The apostle Paul paints a very different picture of God in Romans 12:2. He says God's will is good, pleasing, and perfect. His plans for me are in my best interest. Doing life his way is actually pleasant, satisfying, and enjoyable. His will is perfect; it will never lead me down the wrong path.

Following God isn't about keeping religious rules. It's about a love relationship with the One who redeemed us.

The Christian life is not so much what God wants *from* me as what God wants *for* me. Like any good father, he wants the very best for his children. And—as contrary as it may seem—our best includes *living separate from the world's values.* Our best means that we are different from the world, inside and out. Even our minds are different.

If you don't believe it, put it to the test. Paul says that when you do life God's way—which is different from the world's way—you will be able to test and prove that God's will is good, pleasing, and perfect. It's like Paul is saying, "Take it for a test drive. You'll love how it handles on the road." He has full confidence that if you will follow God's path, you will discover a life that is full, rich, and joyful.

In Romans 12:2 Paul tells us the path to getting God's very best: "Do not conform any longer to the pattern of this world, but be transformed by the renewing of your mind. Then you will be able to test and approve what God's will is—his good, pleasing and perfect will."

Sadly, most Christians don't experience God's very best. Many Christians get conned and seduced into believing the lies of the world and miss out on God's best.

At the heart of "worldliness" is who you love and who you trust to meet the deepest needs of your life.

The Bible says we are in a daily battle with the devil, the flesh, and the world. As Christ-followers, we want to live for Christ. But we live in an environment that is toxic to our spiritual health. So if we don't understand the battle and how our enemy operates, we are destined to spiritual failure and defeat.

Key to winning this daily spiritual battle is to live separate from the world's values. When Paul talks about the world in Romans 12:2, he is not referring to our physical planet. He is referring to a world system that will lead you away from God and into sin. The world's system is a set of beliefs, ideals, and values that compete with God for your love and devotion. First John 2:15–17 helps us understand more fully the world system that God wants us to resist. John says, "Do not love the world or anything in the world. If anyone loves the world, love for the Father is not in them. For everything in the world—the lust of the flesh, the lust of the eyes, and the pride of life—comes not from the Father but from the world. The world and its desires pass away, but whoever does the will of God lives forever" (updated NIV).

In this passage, we discover how sin works in the world system through three basic desires:

- The lust of the flesh = the desire to "feel" (pleasure)
- The lust of the eyes = the desire to "have" (possessions)
- The pride of life = the desire to "be" (position)

The message behind most every commercial can be traced back to one of these three desires. Notice that each of these worldly values is rooted in legitimate needs and longings God has given us. We begin to be conformed to the world when these desires become our focus. They are toxic when our love for them usurps our love for God.

Ultimately, the issue is love. At the heart of "worldliness" is who you love and who you trust to meet the deepest needs of your life. Far too many of us think the Christian life is a list of rules and commandments. As a result, our focus is only on behavior. In *Living on the Edge,* Chip says, "Behavior is almost always only the symptom. The real issue is far deeper. If we would begin to feel deeply sad about running into the arms of another lover and comprehend how deeply this grieves our God who loves us and longs to give us the best, I think we would see a lot more Christians living like Christians."[1]

This week, we'll be looking at a teenager who placed his love for God above his own life. Daniel is a fitting portrait of living separate from the world's values.

WHAT ABOUT YOU?

Before you get back into your day, take a few moments and ask the Holy Spirit to show you if you have been committing spiritual adultery. Is there any place in your heart where the desire for pleasure, possessions, or position has become your first love? The antidote to these kinds of desires is not so much in the discipline of saying no to the world as it is in the desire to say yes to God. It is more about falling in love with God rather than out of love with the world.

Today's Takeaway
At the heart of living separate from the world is the question "Who do you love, and who do you trust to meet your deepest needs?"

day
7

ARE YOU FOLLOWING CHRIST OR THE CROWD?

"**P**ropaganda is a truly terrible weapon in the hands of an expert."[1]

Those words were written by none other than Adolf Hitler. He understood the power of manipulation and deception to accomplish his diabolical objectives. He skillfully manipulated the beliefs and emotions of unsuspecting Germans. His propaganda machine cultivated hatred and suspicion and portrayed the Jews as an enemy to be feared, controlled, and ultimately exterminated. Hitler grasped the power of media to influence people's worldview. Through posters, art, textbooks, films, public rallies, newspapers, and radio, he shaped an entire nation.

Hitler was certainly not the first to grasp the power of brainwashing and manipulating people. Twenty-five hundred years before Hitler, a Babylonian king named Nebuchadnezzar also understood the techniques of shaping people's worldview. Babylon was a world superpower, and its armies were sweeping across the known world conquering nation after nation. Along with their world domination came immorality and idol worship.

In 605 BC Babylon captured Jerusalem. Part of Nebuchadnezzar's strategy was to identify the brightest and best from the countries he conquered and turn them into leaders for Babylon. So he deported some young Hebrews from Jerusalem to Babylon and entered them into a three-year graduate program in brainwashing. Everything for these young men was turned upside down. They were separated from their families and the practices of their Hebrew faith. Their environment, their diet, their language, and their education were all changed in an attempt to make them forget that they were Jews. Their names were even changed to Babylonian names in an attempt to systematically eradicate their past. They were taught a new worldview so that they might embrace the Babylonian culture.

We have God's presence, God's power, and God's truth

But Nebuchadnezzar was not the inventor of brainwashing and manipulation. Thousands of years before Babylon ever came on the scene, Satan invented brainwashing and manipulation. Ever since that moment in the Garden of Eden when Satan said to Eve, "Did God really say . . .?" (Genesis 3:1), he has been manipulating people.

Satan masterfully uses the world system to shape our thinking and challenge our beliefs. Just like Hitler, Satan has a propaganda machine, and he will use every means possible to influence your worldview. He will come at you through movies, talk radio, advertising, websites, education, and a thousand other subtle ways. Every single day you are bombarded with ideas and messages that nudge you to follow the crowd rather than follow Christ. It's like he's holding out a tempting drink with a colorful little umbrella, but the drink is really poison!

We have a powerful enemy who would love to deceive us and brainwash us. That's why in Romans 12:2, the apostle Paul calls us to be separate from the world. He gives a very straightforward command: "Do not conform any longer to the pattern of this world."

Because we have God's presence, God's power, and God's truth, we are not helpless against Satan's attacks. But we must not walk in ignorance. We must be aware of our enemy's strategies. When a football team is getting ready for a big game, they watch lots of film of the opposing team. They want to understand what they are up against.

In 2 Corinthians 2:10, Paul talks about the importance of extending Christ's forgiveness. And then in verse 11, he tells us the reason why: "so that Satan will not outsmart us. For we are familiar with his evil schemes" (2 Corinthians 2:11 NLT). Then, in Ephesians 6:11, Paul challenges us to "Put on all of God's armor so that you will be able to stand firm against all strategies of the devil" (NLT).

The Greek word translated "schemes" and "strategies" is the word from which we get our English word *methods*. In ancient times this word was often used of a wild animal that would stalk and then unexpectedly pounce on its prey.

What a sobering picture of what Satan tries to do in our lives.

WHAT ABOUT YOU?

Spend some time today thinking about some of the ways that Satan seeks to manipulate and brainwash you and your loved ones. Then spend some time seriously pondering the following question: what does it look like practically for you to live separate from the world's values?

Today's Takeaway
*God telling you to live separate from the world's values
is like you telling your kids not to drink poison.*

⌐12

day
8

WHEN TO DRAW A LINE IN THE SAND

In the spring of 1960 a young black man, motivated by deep conviction, decided to take a stand for what he believed was right. It would forever change his life and would also change the course of an entire nation. In those days in South Africa, blacks were not able to vote and they were separated from whites in public businesses. They were forced to live in a small area of the country and couldn't leave that area without a pass. To say the least, tensions ran high during Apartheid.

So in 1960, in protest against the inequities of Apartheid, Nelson Mandela burned his pass.

In 1962, Mandela was arrested and imprisoned for trying to overthrow the government. He spent twenty-seven years behind bars, but he continued the fight from his prison cell. In 1993, three years after his release, Mandela earned the Nobel Peace Prize for his work in improving human rights. In 1994, Nelson Mandela became the first black South African to be elected president of his country.[1]

> We all face moments when we have to decide whether or not we will stand up for our convictions.

Though they may not be as dramatic as those in Nelson Mandela's journey, we all face moments when we have to decide whether or not we will stand up for our convictions.

In the Old Testament we read about one such defining moment in the life of a young Hebrew named Daniel. Try to imagine this scene. Babylon had captured Jerusalem. Along with the typical spoils of war, King Nebuchadnezzar also carried back to Babylon some of Jerusalem's brightest and best young men. They soon found that the idol-worshipping Babylonians had no interest or regard for the God of Israel.

Daniel wasn't in Babylon long before his first conflict of faith presented itself. Being trained in the king's palace meant eating the king's food and drinking the king's wine. But Daniel likely knew that this meat had also been offered to idols and he would have compromised his conviction to eat it. How could he as a fifteen- or sixteen-year-old kid stand up to the king?

Daniel decided in advance to be obedient and to trust God with the consequences.

Before we go any further, think about this question. What would you have done if you had been Daniel? Most of us probably would have rationalized, "It's not worth making a big deal over." Or we would have said, "I don't really have a choice. I'm just a teenager, and no one back home is going to know anyway."

But Daniel had a different response. In Daniel 1:8, the Bible says, "Daniel resolved not to defile himself." Notice the word "resolved." Daniel drew a line in the sand. He drove a stake in the ground.

A teenager taking on the great Babylonian king displays incredible courage. Daniel had no way of knowing what the consequences would be. His decision could have cost him his life. But he refused to compromise. Daniel decided in advance to be obedient and to trust God with the consequences.

WHAT ABOUT YOU?

Only by personal study and digging into the Word of God will faith really become yours. As you personally search the Bible and discover what God says about the key issues of life, you will separate out your opinions from your biblical convictions.

So how about it? Are you clear about your convictions? Have you settled the nonnegotiables of your life? Are you prepared to draw a line in the sand?

Today's Takeaway

Courageous conduct flows out of clear convictions.

day
9

DON'T BE A JERK FOR JESUS

"What a bunch of jerks." Those were the words put on a huge billboard by Christ Covenant Church in Beaumont, Texas.[1] What a bunch of jerks. Prideful, hypocritical, selfish, judgmental jerks.

It was a self-indictment of Christians and the way we are often perceived.

Ghandi would have agreed. He said, "I like your Christ; I do not like your Christians. Your Christians are so unlike your Christ."

Pastor Chris Beard said of the billboard, "We wanted to reach out to the community and send the message that as a church we messed up—and it looks like we've got people's attention. Really, we want a chance to say that all the things people say about Christians can be true, and we want to change that. At Christ Covenant Church, do you know what our response is? Guilty as charged. We are fed up with it just as much as you are. We've failed. We've failed you, we've failed each other, and the worst part is that we've failed to act like Jesus."[2]

A lot of damage has been done to the cause of Christ by people who took a stand for their Christian convictions in an unchristian way. Grumpy, mean-spirited, cranky Christians have caused the world to look at us and say, "What a bunch of jerks."

We could learn a lot from Daniel about how to stand for our convictions and to do so in a gracious manner. As a teenager, he was taken from his family and his home. By the edict of King Nebuchadnezzar, he was deported to Babylon. As an elite and promising leader, he spent the next three years getting an education in Babylonian language, literature, and culture. All of this training was to prepare Daniel for service to the king.

In the kingdom of God, conviction and kindness go hand in hand.

One of the perks of being in the king's training program was that you got to eat from the royal menu. You ate royal steak and drank the best wine in the land. This was a problem for Daniel. It wasn't because Daniel was a teetotaler or a vegetarian. The problem was that this wine and meat was being offered to idols. For Daniel to partake would be to indirectly participate in idol worship. So he went to the head official and said, "The diet you have prepared for us violates what we believe. So how about giving us a different diet—just vegetables and water?"

The official said, "I can't do that. If you Hebrew guys aren't looking fit, I'll get blamed. The king will have my head."

Notice Daniel's response. He didn't get antagonistic or belligerent. He didn't become a jerk. He simply offered a possible solution: "Give us a ten-day test, eating only vegetables and drinking only water."

Daniel's response was gracious, marked by kindness and courtesy. What a great lesson for believers in the twenty-first century. It doesn't just matter what we stand for; it matters how we take our stand.

Notice the word *gracious* in the three verses below.

- Proverbs 16:24: "Gracious words are a honeycomb, sweet to the soul and healing to the bones" (updated NIV).
- Proverbs 15:26: "The LORD detests the thoughts of the wicked, but gracious words are pure in his sight" (updated NIV).
- Luke 4:22: "All spoke well of him and were amazed at the gracious words that came from his lips. 'Isn't this Joseph's son?' they asked."

We read several times in Scripture that when Jesus spoke, he spoke as one having authority. But in this passage in Luke, his words are described as *gracious*. Jesus was winsome and endearing. He had a gentleness about him that drew people to him.

To truly live separate from the world, we must model both truth and grace. We must courageously stand for truth, we must resist the world system, and we must do so graciously. In the kingdom of God, conviction and kindness stand together.

WHAT ABOUT YOU?

Are you modeling both truth and grace in your life? Is your speech gracious and kind, or do you tend to sound more like a jerk? As you surrender your life to Christ and commit to living separate from the world's values, God will shape your heart—and your speech. And before long, people will be describing you as *gracious*.

Today's Takeaway
It doesn't just matter what you stand for;
it matters how you take your stand.

⏸12

day
10

SAYING NO
REQUIRES A HIGHER YES

Tony Blair, former British prime minister, once said, "The art of leadership is saying no, not yes. It is very easy to say yes."[1] His insight is not only true about people who lead organizations and nations and churches; it's also true of people who lead themselves well.

God has commanded us to live separate from the world's values, and that means we have to learn how to say no. The world system in which we live is usually opposed to the ways of God. In other words, the values of culture are in conflict with the values of God. James doesn't pull any punches when he talks about the incompatibility of the world's ways and God's ways: "You adulterers! Don't you realize that friendship with the world makes you an enemy of God?" (James 4:4 NLT).

But let's be honest: saying no to the world is not easy. Even as a Christ-follower, it's a daily battle to choose God's ways over the world's ways. The world system is seductive and alluring.

Here is the key to victory: saying no requires a higher yes. My ability to say no to the world is connected to my desire to say yes to God. I say yes to the belief that God's way is right and best for me. Saying yes to an intimate relationship with my heavenly Father, helps me to say no to anything that could damage that relationship.

That's why when Paul challenges us not to be conformed to the world, he immediately challenges us to be transformed by renewing our minds (Romans 12:2). We are able to say no to the world because our higher yes is that we want the mind of Christ.

Daniel serves as a great example of this truth. By chapter 6, Daniel was one of the top three political leaders in the entire kingdom of Babylon. This caused jealousy among other political leaders, and they began to look for a way to discredit Daniel.

There was just one problem. They couldn't dig up any dirt on Daniel. His integrity was impeccable. Daniel 6:4 says, "They could find no corruption in him, because he was trustworthy and neither corrupt nor negligent."

Daniel definitely lived separate from the Babylonian world system. So these political adversaries devised a plot to bring him down. They knew the one thing Daniel wouldn't compromise was his relationship with God. They got the king to sign an edict that for thirty days people could only pray to the king.

Interestingly, Daniel's enemies were absolutely right: Daniel wasn't about to compromise his cherished prayer times with his heavenly Father. "But when Daniel learned that the law had been signed, he went home and knelt down as usual in his upstairs room, with its windows open toward Jerusalem. He prayed three times a day, just as he had always done, giving thanks to his God." (Daniel 6:10 NLT).

Daniel's obedience to God meant disobedience to the king and landed him in the lions' den. Even

> Saying yes to an intimate relationship with my heavenly Father, helps me to say no to anything that could damage that relationship.

though he spent the entire night surrounded by lions, he was not harmed. At the first light of dawn, the king rushed to the lions' den to see if, by some miracle, Daniel's God had rescued him.

Notice Daniel's words. He said, "O king, live forever! My God sent his angel, and he shut the mouths of the lions" (Daniel 6:21). Daniel didn't say, "The great creator God has spared me." No, his response is far more personal. "*My* God, the God I spend time with every day, has rescued me."

What gave Daniel courage to live separate from the world around him was his relationship with God. His deep communion with God led to deep conviction about God, which resulted in deep courage for God.

WHAT ABOUT YOU?

What distractions or temptations from the world keep you from a more intimate relationship with God? If you want to learn how to say no to the seductions of the world system, you begin by saying yes to a pure and intimate relationship with God—and that means that, just like Daniel, you'll protect your times of prayer and fellowship with your heavenly Father.

Today's Takeaway
Saying no to the world is connected to
your desire to say yes to God.

🔊12

part 3

Sober in Self-Assessment

MOSES

Do not think of yourself more highly than you ought,

but rather think of yourself with sober judgment,

in accordance with the faith

God has distributed to each of you.

—Romans 12:3 updated niv

true spirituality

day
11

SPIRITUAL
IDENTITY THEFT

The Bourne Identity is a 2002 American spy film that tells the story of Jason Bourne, who is entangled in a CIA conspiracy. But there's a twist: Jason doesn't know his name. He doesn't know where he came from. He doesn't know if he has any family. He has incredible hand-to-hand combat skills but has no idea how he acquired them. Jason suffers from retrograde amnesia. The movie is really about his desperate attempt to discover his true identity.

Inside every person on the planet, there is a deep longing to discover our true identities. Human beings (either consciously or subconsciously) are always seeking the answers to three fundamental questions in life. Chip Ingram has this insightful list in his book *Living on the Edge*:

1. *Who am I?* This question deals with our identity.
2. *Where do I belong?* This question deals with our security.
3. *What am I supposed to do?* This question deals with our significance.[1]

These are good questions, and we find some answers in Romans 12.

1. Who are you?

For by the grace given me I say to every one of you: Do not think
of yourself more highly than you ought, but rather think of yourself
with sober judgment, in accordance with the faith God has distributed to each of you. (Romans 12:3 updated NIV)

The main point of verse 3 is that we are to think accurately about ourselves. An important root word is repeated four times in this one verse, as
shown with the emphasized words below:

For by the grace given me I say to every one of you: Do not *think*
of yourself more highly than you *ought*, but rather *think* of yourself
with *sober judgment*, in accordance with the faith God has distributed to each of you. (Romans 12:3 updated NIV; emphasis added)

Each time this root word is used, it is a call from God to think clearly
and accurately about who we are. Because of personal baggage, deep in-
security, or past hurts, we often carry around a distorted view of who we
really are.

One of the best days you will ever have is the day you finally realize who
you are in Christ. One translation of Ephesians 2:10 says, "We are God's
masterpiece" (NLT). Let that sink in. No matter what skeletons are in your
closet, you are God's masterpiece. It is liberating to realize that God doesn't
see me through my past, but through Jesus.

When I begin to grasp this truth, I won't think too lowly of myself
because I will know that I matter and am deeply loved by the great God of
the universe. And I won't think too highly of myself because I know that
everything I have and am is by God's grace.

2. Where do you belong?

For just as each of us has one body with many members, and these members do not all have the same function, so in Christ we, though many, form one body, and each member belongs to all the others. (Romans 12:4–5 updated NIV)

All of us need to belong. Even the most independent individualist longs for belonging. None of us can live the Christian life alone. We need not only the Holy Spirit, but we need other people. That is why this passage says that God has connected us to his church—the body of Christ.

But we are not only called to *connect*, but also to *contribute*. Each of us has a role to fulfill. You are needed. A good question to ask yourself is, "What are my top strengths, and how am I using them to serve God and others?"

3. What are you supposed to do?

We have different gifts, according to the grace given to each of us. (Romans 12:6 updated NIV)

Romans 12:6 is the secret to discovering our place in life and in the body of Christ. We are each supposed to discover and deploy our spiritual gifts. God has deposited into each believer a supernatural ability to help build up the body of Christ.

Identifying your spiritual gift will give you a primary indicator of what God wants you to do with your life. It will help you know what to say yes to and what to say no to. It will help you know where

> God has deposited into each believer a supernatural ability to help build up the body of Christ.

to spend your time and energy. As Chip writes, "Knowing your primary spiritual gift can turn the spiritual flashlight of your focus into a spiritual laser beam."[2]

As you'll see in the rest of this week's devotionals, Moses was a man who struggled to discover his identity and how he fit into God's plan. With the tenacity of Jason Bourne, may you discover your true identity and what it is that God has gifted you to do with your life.

WHAT ABOUT YOU?

Today's devotion probably gave you a lot to think about, and you may not be able to process it all at once, but spend some today pondering the three universal questions: *Who am I? Where do I belong?* and *What am I supposed to do?* What did you learn about yourself as you read? What ideas do you want to explore further? Once you begin to answer these three questions, you'll feel more confident in God's love, you'll begin to find a place to belong, and you'll be on your way to figuring out how God wants you to use the gifts he's given you.

Today's Takeaway
God doesn't see me through my past,
he sees me through Jesus.

day
12

GOD NEVER
WASTES A HURT

Going through security at the airport can be about as much fun as a root canal. You probably know the drill. You check in at the counter, get your boarding pass, and then head off to the security line. After having your boarding pass and ID checked several times—and after taking off your shoes, coat, belt, watch, and keys—you are ready for the final part of the screening process: you put your carry-on bag through the security machine.

As your bag goes through the machine, a security agent peers intently at a screen that reveals the contents of your bag. The agent carefully scans your personal and private items looking for anything dangerous. He sees what no one else can. And then if he finds anything suspicious-looking on the screen, he sets your bag aside and looks through it manually. Honestly, it can be a little uncomfortable for someone to look inside our baggage.

What's true at the airport is also true in life. Every one of us carries around a backpack full of stuff we would rather keep hidden. Past hurts, painful and shameful experiences, destructive habits, broken relationships, secret sin, unfulfilled dreams . . . these are the things that fill our backpacks.

Whether we realize it or not, what we carry around in our backpack impacts how we see ourselves and how we respond to God.

Even a great Bible character like Moses had a backpack. Moses was born a Hebrew, but by God's providence he became the adopted son of Pharaoh's daughter. He lived a pampered and promising life, until one moment of rage changed his life forever. One day, at the age of forty, he saw an Egyptian beating a Hebrew. Enraged, Moses did the unthinkable: he murdered the Egyptian and hid his body in the sand.

Sometimes the experiences we are most ashamed of are the very things God wants to use as our ministry to others.

What Moses thought he'd done in secret became known the very next day, and he had to run for his life. In one day he went from being a favored son in the palace to being a fugitive in the desert. He landed in a place called Midian where he became a common shepherd. The last eleven verses of Exodus 2 cover forty years of Moses life. All we know of those forty years is that Moses got married, had a son, and tended sheep for his father-in-law. During those years, his days were filled with routine and mundane tasks, and he had plenty of time to reflect on how he'd blown it.

By the time God met him in the burning bush, Moses was eighty years old. He had a backpack full of "stuff" that made him feel inadequate for the assignment God gave him of leading the people out of the bondage of Egypt.

All of Moses' past—the good, the bad, the ugly—had been used by a sovereign God to prepare Moses for his divine assignment. But Moses didn't see it that way, and he felt unable to do what God called him to do.

Moses didn't yet understand that his past had prepared him for his future. To lead the Israelites out of Egypt, he would need to know all about Egypt and Pharaoh and the pagan gods they served. Moses would need a great education. Moses would need to know how to navigate life in the desert. Moses' failures would help him depend more on God than himself.

And here's what you need to understand. God sovereignly uses your parents, your background, your physical DNA, your hardships, your talents, and even your failures. Sometimes the experiences we are most ashamed of are the very things God wants to use as our ministry to others. God never wastes a hurt.

Notice the words of the apostle Paul as he describes his past and how God used it to help people see that no matter what they had done, they were not beyond the reach of God's grace.

This is a trustworthy saying, and everyone should accept it: "Christ Jesus came into the world to save sinners"—and I am the worst of them all. But God had mercy on me so that Christ Jesus could use me as a prime example of his great patience with even the worst sinners. Then others will realize that they, too, can believe in him and receive eternal life. (1 Timothy 1:15–16 NLT)

Understanding your past helps inform your future. Your past experiences are the breadcrumbs leading you to discover how God will use you in the future.

WHAT ABOUT YOU?

What about your past gives clues to your gifts and passions? Remember, God never wastes a hurt. What treasures has God pulled out of your pain? Spend some time thinking and praying about this today.

Today's Takeaway

Your past experiences are the breadcrumbs leading you to discover God's plan for your future.

day

13

EXCUSE ME

The following are actual excuses sent from parents to their kids' teachers:

- Dear School, Please excuse my son from being absent on Jan. 29, 30, 31, 32, and also 33.
- My son is under a doctor's care and should not take PE today. Please execute him.
- Please excuse my daughter from Jim class for a few days. Yesterday she fell out of a tree and misplaced her hip.
- Please excuse my son. He will be out next week slaughtering goats for his manhood ritual. Thank you!
- The basement of our house got flooded where the children sleep so they had to be vaporized.[1]

No one has to teach us how to make excuses. It seems as though we come factory-installed with this crafty skill. We make excuses to bosses, spouses, kids, coaches, friends, teachers, and even God.

Moses is a classic case study in making excuses. When Moses was eighty God met him at the burning bush. God gave him the assignment of delivering the Israelites out of the slavery of Egypt and leading them to the Promised Land (Exodus 3:7–10). But Moses had lived as a fugitive for the last forty years in absolute obscurity. His life back in the Egyptian palace was nothing more than a faded memory. He was no longer the up-and-coming prince of Egypt. He was a shepherd on the backside of the desert. So coming up with excuses why he wasn't a good candidate for the job flowed easily and freely off of his lips.

Moses' first excuse came in the form of a question: "Who am I?" (Exodus 3:11). But it wasn't really a question. It was a statement of inadequacy and fear. Moses was basically saying, "I'm a nobody."

It's interesting that God didn't try to bolster Moses' self-esteem. God isn't as interested in our self-esteem as he is our surrender. God's response wasn't about Moses at all; it was about himself. His answer to Moses' question was, "I will be with you" (Exodus 3:12). It's like God was saying, *Moses, you're right. You are inadequate, but this isn't about your skill and ability. My presence and power is what you need.*

> God isn't as interested in our self-esteem as he is our surrender.

Another excuse Moses pulled out of his bag that day had to do with his perceived lack of credibility: "What if they do not believe me or listen to me and say 'The LORD did not appear to you'?" (Exodus 4:1).

Rather than moving out based on the clear call of God, Moses started anticipating all the problems he might encounter. He envisioned going back to Egypt only to be rejected. But God rarely shows us the whole plan. He gives us just enough to get started and then says, *Trust me.*

This occasion with Moses was no different. God didn't tell Moses how the plan would work; he just demonstrated how his power could work through who Moses already was. God's response? "What is that in your hand?" (Exodus 4:2). He turned Moses' staff into a snake and then back into a staff again. Then he turned Moses' hand leprous and then whole again. God used Moses' shepherd's staff and his own hand to demonstrate his irrefutable power.

Notice what God said to Moses next: "'This,' said the LORD, 'is so that they may believe that the LORD, the God of their fathers—the God of Abraham, the God of Isaac and the God of Jacob—has appeared to you'" (Exodus 4:5).

In essence, God was saying, "Your credibility isn't the issue. Trust me, and get your focus off yourself. I'll take what you already have and, by my power and my grace, I'll use you in ways that you never dreamed."

In a last-ditch effort to resist God's assignment, Moses claimed he didn't have the needed skill. "Moses said to the LORD, 'Pardon your servant, Lord. I have never been eloquent, neither in the past nor since you have spoken to your servant. I am slow of speech and tongue'" (Exodus 4:10 updated NIV). In other words, "I don't have the skill it takes to succeed. Get someone else to do it."

Once again God just asserts his sovereignty. "The LORD said, "Who gave human beings their mouths? Who makes them deaf or mute? Who gives them sight or makes them blind? Is it not I, the LORD? Now go; I will help you speak and will teach you what to say" (Exodus 4:11 updated NIV).

Here is the lesson Moses had a hard time accepting: his past experience, his gifts, and the power of God were all that he needed.

WHAT ABOUT YOU?

As you reflect on your life, have you been offering God any of the same excuses as Moses? When called upon to contribute to God's purposes, have you asked:

- *"Who am I?"* Remember God's answer: *I will be with you.*
- Or maybe you've felt you lack credibility and said, *They won't believe me.* God says to you just what he said to Moses: *What is that in your hand?* He has already equipped you with valuable gifts.
- Finally, maybe you've desperately said, *"I can't do it! Please, get someone else!"* God's answer to you is, *I will help you and teach you what to say.*

Today's Takeaway
God using you isn't as much about your ability as it is your availability.

THE HARDEST PERSON FOR YOU TO LEAD IS . . . YOU

We all have our blind spots. And we all have the uncanny ability to be self-deceived. The actor Daniel Day-Lewis said this about self-delusion: "I suppose I have a highly developed capacity for self-delusion, so it's no problem for me to believe that I'm somebody else."

You would think that knowing yourself and thinking accurately about yourself would be easy. After all, we spend more time with ourselves than anybody else. We certainly think about ourselves more than we think about anybody else. We have a front-row seat to our private thoughts as well as our public actions.

But the truth is we have an amazing ability to self-deceive. That's why the hardest person you will ever lead is *you*. Jesus' harshest criticism was reserved for Pharisees who were living in self-deceit. All of us possess distorted thinking and blind spots. What we sometimes can't see in us, others see easily.

If we want to see ourselves accurately we'll need the help of others. Moses' father-in-law, Jethro, played such a role in the life of Moses.

Picture this scene: By God's miraculous power, Moses had successfully led the people of Israel out of Egypt. Two million of them were moving through the desert on their way to the Promised Land. God was supernaturally feeding them with manna and quail.

Moses' wife and sons have been staying with her parents. But now that the Israelites were safely out of Egypt and in the desert, Jethro brought Zipporah and the boys to Moses. It was a wonderful time of reunion and celebration and sharing news of God's powerful deliverance.

The Bible says, "The next day Moses took his seat to serve as judge for the people, and they stood around him from morning till evening" (Exodus 18:13). Moses was the lone judge, dispute-settler, and decision-maker for the entire two-million-member nation.

It's no wonder that Jethro looked at this scene and told Moses, "This is crazy!" That's a loose translation, but you get the gist of it. He told Moses that what he was doing was not good. In fact, he told Moses, you're going to wear yourself out, and you're going to wear the people out (Exodus 18:17–18).

Jethro basically told Moses, "What you're doing is not the best use of you, and it's not best for the people. You are not operating in your sweet spot." Moses needed a different plan that would maximize his gifts and contribution and more effectively meet the needs of the people.

Jethro suggested Moses focus on three things: praying for the people, teaching them how to live, and finding capable men who could manage the problems and make good decisions (Exodus 18:19–20). This solution was a win-win. Jethro said, "If you do this and God so commands, you will be able to stand the strain, and all these people will go home satisfied" (Exodus 18:23).

Moses was oblivious to what was obvious to Jethro. That day Jethro gave Moses and the entire nation of Israel a tremendous gift. His advice allowed

Moses to operate in his sweet spot, and it opened the way for others to use their God-given gifts. The passage says that Moses listened to Jethro and did everything he said.

We all need people in our lives who love us enough to tell us the truth. Solomon was right—"An honest answer is like a kiss on the lips" (Proverbs 24:26). Solomon also said, "He who listens to a life-giving rebuke will be at home among the wise" (Proverbs 15:31).

> We all need people in our lives who love us enough to tell us the truth.

Moses was wise to listen to the advice of his father-in-law. It would have been easy for Moses to become defensive—and many of us would. He could have told Jethro, "I'm the God-appointed leader. I know what is best." But he didn't. He was wise enough and humble enough to listen to the counsel of someone who loved him and wanted the best for Moses and the people.

WHAT ABOUT YOU?

Who have you invited to honestly speak into your life? Do you have anyone who tells you what you *need* to hear, not just what you want to hear? Just like Moses, you have blind spots. You, too, need the help of others to make sure you are maximizing your strengths and augmenting your weaknesses. You'll be better for it.

Today's Takeaway
You are often oblivious to what is obvious to others.

๑12

IT'S ABOUT GOD'S PRESENCE, NOT HIS PRESENTS

"**S**o many people have asked what is next for me, and the truth is I have no idea. My first commitment is to my relationship with Jesus Christ. I am so far away from the man I was when I first felt the call to start my church. I've become all about me and my ego. I have to focus on getting my walk with God where it should be before I can do anything else."[1]

Those painful words are from a young and rising megachurch pastor who fell into moral sin and had to step down from his church. In recent years, we've seen a steady stream of scandals among well-known and gifted pastors. The story that hits the headlines is always about the scandalous and shocking behavior. However, there's another story that is rarely mentioned. It is the story of a neglected soul and mismanaged character. It's the story of a subtle and slow disconnect from Jesus.

These personal and ministry tragedies serve as a good reminder of what each of us is capable of. Even when we have incredible gifts and have known the Lord for a long time, we can still lose our way.

In fact, the longer we walk with God, the more susceptible to the danger of self-reliance we become. We may begin to rely on our ability, our gifts (God's "presents"), and our experience. Part of having a sober self-assessment is being self-aware of our sinfulness and our need for Christ.

Even when we have incredible gifts and have known the Lord for a long time, we can still lose our way.

When we lose sight of this truth, we can actually hijack our God-given gifts. We can start thinking that our gifts are because of us and for us. Instead of holding them loosely as a gift of God's grace, we cling to them and are filled with pride. That's why Paul doesn't pull any punches in Romans 12:3 when he says, "Do not think of yourself more highly than you ought."

We see an interesting progression in the life of Moses that reminds us of the importance of staying connected to Jesus. As we talked about in day 13, when God came to Moses at the burning bush and gave him the assignment of leading the people of Israel out of Egypt, Moses had a predictable response: "Who am I, that I should go to Pharaoh and bring the Israelites out of Egypt?" (Exodus 3:11).

God's answer to Moses' question was not spectacular or dramatic. God simply said, "I will be with you" (Exodus 3:12).

God said the people would follow Moses because he had the presence of God in his life. That is what qualified him for spiritual leadership of the people. It wasn't because Moses was the brightest, the most skilled, or had the most winsome personality. The one characteristic that would give his leadership credibility and spiritual power was God's presence.

But that wasn't enough for Moses. He wanted something more tangible, more dazzling, and more spectacular. So God did the miracles with Moses' staff becoming a snake and his hand becoming leprous. He even gave Aaron to Moses as a mouthpiece to help with communication.

If you skip ahead thirty chapters to Exodus 33, you will find a very different scene. Moses had interceded for the Israelites and asked God not to destroy them because of their idolatry. God answered by saying he would send them into the Promised Land but that his presence wouldn't go with them. In Exodus 33:3, God tells us why: "I will not go with you, because you are a stiff-necked people and I might destroy you on the way."

Moses' response to God gives us a clue about how far his relationship with God had developed over the years since the burning-bush encounter. He had matured, and his soul was deeply connected to God. "Then Moses said to him, 'If your Presence does not go with us, do not send us up from here'" (Exodus 33:15).

In Exodus 3, God's presence wasn't enough for Moses. He needed the dramatic and spectacular. But by Exodus 33, God's presence was all that mattered to Moses. God was his life. Moses had learned the valuable lesson that his relationship with God mattered more than his skill and leadership.

WHAT ABOUT YOU?

Are you tempted to elevate your own gifts above your dependence on God? If you have been a long-time Christ follower, this is a very real temptation. Now is a good time for a sober self-assessment to remember that we are nothing outside of God's presence. We can be encouraged as we look at the life of Moses. When he began his journey toward the Promised Land with God and the Israelites, he had no comprehension of the power that resided in God's presence alone. But as he grew in faith, God's presence was all that mattered to him.

Today's Takeaway

Seek God's presence more than his provision.

☙12

part 4

serving in love

JONATHAN

Love must be sincere.

Hate what is evil; cling to what is good.

Be devoted to one another in love.

Honor one another above yourselves.

—Romans 12:9–10

day 16

LONE RANGER CHRISTIANS NEED NOT APPLY

A few years ago, we moved to a new town and a new church. My son had just finished high school but hadn't started college. My son is a bit of an introvert, and we were concerned about how well he would connect in this new and much larger church. After being there a couple of weeks, he decided to check out the Thursday night college service. I happened to be on campus that night and decided to drop by and see if my son was there. By the time I arrived, the college pastor was already speaking. I really wasn't interested in what he had to say. I was interested in whether my son was there. I stood back by the soundboard scanning the room looking for my son—and then I spotted him. He was sitting to the left about two-thirds of the way back . . . all by himself. My heart sank. I wanted to stand up and shout, "Will somebody please reach out to my kid?" As a father, I wanted my son to find relationships and a sense of belonging. Our heavenly Father desires the same.

Living the Christian life in isolation is not an option. In fact, it's not an overstatement to say that you can't live the Christian life by yourself. There is no such thing as Lone Ranger Christianity. The Bible urges us to be meaningfully connected to other believers. Not just sitting next to them in a church service, but actually in their lives, experiencing authentic community.

Jesus even gave the world the right to judge the authenticity of our faith based on how well we love each other. He said, "By this everyone will know that you are my disciples, if you love one another" (John 13:35 updated NIV).

You see, from the very beginning God has wired us for relationship. The first time God ever said anything was *not* good, he said, "It is not good for the man to be alone" (Genesis 2:18). That verse is often used to talk about marriage, but more fundamentally, it shows us that God wired us for relationship.

In fact, our lives are defined by relationships. Generally speaking, life's most exhilarating, heart-pounding highs and life's most gut-wrenching, painful lows come from relationships. When you walk into somebody's home and look at the pictures on their fireplace mantle, they are not photos of houses, cars, jewelry, or their bank. They are photos of people. This is a bold reminder that life's meaning is largely derived from relationships.

But relationships are messy. Someone has said the Christian life would be easy if it weren't for people. It's true. Getting along with and loving other Christians is no small challenge. You may also have heard the famous saying: "To dwell above with those we love, that would be the glory. To dwell below with those we know, well that's a different story!"

To do relationships well takes a lot of devotion and skill. So, here's the question: how do we take authentic community from the romantic notion of relationships in the "sweet by and by" to actually living it out in the "nasty here and now"?

In Romans 12:9–13, the apostle Paul provides some very practical instructions on what it looks like to live in authentic community.

Love must be sincere. Hate what is evil; cling to what is good. Be devoted to one another in brotherly love. Honor one another above yourselves. Never be lacking in zeal, but keep your spiritual fervor, serving the Lord. Be joyful in hope, patient in affliction, faithful in prayer. Share with God's people who are in need. Practice hospitality.

Chip Ingram says about this passage: "Authentic community occurs when the real you (v.9) meets real needs (v. 10) for the right reason (v. 11) in the right way (vv. 12-13)."[1]

The word translated "sincere" in verse 9 literally means 'without a mask'. For authentic community to occur, we have to take off our masks. If there is a singular disease that ruins authentic community, it is hypocrisy. True community involves being open, honest, and appropriately vulnerable. Because of our fear of rejection, this level of honesty sometimes feels very risky. But we can never truly be loved unless people know who we really are. Being "real" is a nonnegotiable for authentic community.

Then in verse 10, Paul challenges us to "be devoted to one another in brotherly love." We are to love and treat other people in the body of Christ as we would our own flesh and blood family. Paul then goes on to explain what he means by being "devoted" to one another. He says that devotion demands that we "honor one another" above ourselves. It literally means 'outdoing one another' in giving honor.

We can never truly be loved unless people know who we really are.

Paul concludes this passage on community with very tangible evidence. In verses 12 and 13, he tells us that authentic community occurs when we share with those in need and practice the art of hospitality. Paul says community is more than verbal concern and emotional support. True community sometimes means getting out our wallets and financially sacrificing to meet a need. Everything we have belongs to God, and he often wants to use us as the conduit through which he blesses others.

We read in Acts 4:32, "All the believers were one in heart and mind. No one claimed that any of their possessions was their own, but they shared everything they had" (updated NIV).

What an incredible testimony to authentic community. The Bible characters we'll look at this week are also extraordinary testimonies to real community. The love and friendship between David and Jonathan present a real-life picture of the community Paul talks about in Romans 12. Theirs was the kind of friendship that laid *everything* on the line.

WHAT ABOUT YOU?

Are you personally experiencing the kind of community Paul describes in Romans 12? If not, resolve this week to begin to pursue it. Don't wait for it to come to you . . . take the initiative.

Today's Takeaway

Being "real" is essential for "real community" to take place.

⊙12

day 17

YOU'VE GOT A FRIEND

In his book *Bowling Alone,* Robert Putnam identifies what he believes is the number one need in America today. He calls loneliness the new American epidemic.[1]

Never in the history of the world have we had more options for staying connected technologically, yet so many still struggle to be connected relationally. It is God's plan for you to be connected both vertically (in relationship to him) and horizontally (in relationship with other believers).

Jonathan and David serve as a great example of the kind of friendship God desires us to have. When Jonathan and David met, they came from different sides of the tracks and had very little in common. David was a poor shepherd; Jonathan was a prince, the next in line to be king of Israel. Yet in spite of their differences, they became fast friends: "After David had finished talking with Saul, he met Jonathan, the king's son. There was an immediate bond between them, for Jonathan loved David" (1 Samuel 18:1 NLT).

Jonathan was intentional in his pursuit of friendship with David. "And Jonathan made a solemn pact with David, because he loved him as he loved himself. Jonathan sealed the pact by taking off his robe and giving it to David, together with his tunic, sword, bow, and belt" (1 Samuel

18:3–4 NLT). You don't see this kind of openness very often, especially between men. Jonathan openly declared his commitment to his friendship with David. He took seriously his need for relational connection. And to seal that friendship, Jonathan gave David the very clothes off his back.

To truly experience authentic community requires initiative.

To have a friend, you must be a friend. To truly experience authentic community requires initiative.

Passivity is the enemy of deep friendship. If friendship is important to you—and remember, it's important to God—then get after it. Be proactive. Don't sit by the phone waiting for it to ring. Be persistent. Pursue relationship and don't give up. You need to own this for yourself.

I hope this goes without saying, but we shouldn't pursue a relationship to the extent that we become a pest. Not everyone will have the time or desire to pursue friendship with us. That's okay. But don't give up on making friends. Reach out to someone else. You will never drift into deep friendship. It takes intentionality and it takes time.

One of the major barriers to authentic community is our twenty-first-century pace of life. The result is that we start skimming relationally. Most of us would not debate the necessity of life-giving relationships. We have good intentions about becoming a part of such relationships, but our busy lives always seem to push this priority to the fringe.

One of the reasons the early church was so powerful was because the Bible says they met together daily (Acts 2:46). They spent time together.

John Ortberg says, "We try to create first-century community on a twenty-first-century timetable . . . and it doesn't work."[2] There are no shortcuts to authentic community.

You can't go deep in a hurry. You can't listen in a hurry. You can't walk through a crisis in a hurry. You can't celebrate in a hurry. You can't savor life in a hurry. If you think you can fit a real relationship in around the edges of an already packed schedule, think again!

You can't go deep with everybody, but you can with a few.

WHAT ABOUT YOU?

Maybe you need to get more intentional about relationship and even declare your commitment to go deep with a handful of friends. Maybe you need to sit down over lunch with someone this week and let him or her know that you want to take the relationship deeper.

Today's Takeaway

You will never drift into authentic
community. It takes intentionality.

day

18

DO YOU HAVE
A 2 A.M. FRIEND?

"If you had a crisis at 2 a.m., who would you call?" Ponder that question for just a moment. Who would you call? Does a name or two come to mind? That was the question posed to a group of men at an elders' retreat.

Each of the men at the retreat mentioned the names of old army buddies, guys they played sports with, college frat brothers, or family members. But surprisingly, not one elder mentioned the name of another man in the room or another man in the church. What was clear was that the relationships among the men in the church were polite but superficial.

The kind of authentic community Jesus desires among believers includes developing some 2 a.m. friends. That will never happen if our Christian friendships are limited to casual conversation at the church on Sundays. It takes intentionality to pursue deeper relationships beyond Sunday. Being a 2 a.m. friend takes time. And it takes getting real and open about your life.

David and Jonathan definitely had a 2 a.m. friend-

> Being a 2 a.m. friend takes time. And it takes getting real and open about your life.

ship. If you are a 2 a.m. friend, below is some evidence of that kind of friendship. Being a 2 a.m. friend is a treasured service of love.

You Come to Your Friend's Defense

A 2 a.m. friend protects his friend and doesn't let other people hurt him. First Samuel 19:1–2 says "Saul now urged his servants and his son Jonathan to assassinate David. But Jonathan, because of his strong affection for David, told him what his father was planning. 'Tomorrow morning,' he warned him, 'you must find a hiding place out in the fields'" (NLT).

You probably won't have to protect your friends from physical persecution, but you will have to protect them in conversations.

You Speak Well of Your Friend When He's Not Around

First Samuel 19:4 says, "The next morning Jonathan spoke with his father about David, saying many good things about him. 'The king must not sin against his servant David,' Jonathan said. 'He's never done anything to harm you. He has always helped you in any way he could'" (NLT).

Notice the phrase "saying many good things about him." What a gift to have a friend you can always trust to speak well of you.

You Are There for Him in Times of Crisis

When Saul once again tried to kill David, Jonathan found David and said, "Tell me what I can do to help you" (1 Samuel 20:4 NLT).

Solomon talks about this kind of friendship in the book of Proverbs: "A man of many companions may come to ruin, but there is a friend who sticks closer than a brother" (Proverbs 18:24).

This is the friend you know will be there for you no matter what the situation. You don't have to prove yourself to a 2 a.m. friend. You don't have to impress him, you don't have to get him to like you, you don't have to wonder if he is on your team, and you don't have to worry about what he says about you when you're not around.

You Are Totally Honest with a 2 a.m. Friend

By the time you get to 1 Samuel 20, David was desperate and frantic. Jonathan's father, King Saul, was relentlessly trying to have him killed. David was literally running for his life. So he turned to his friend Jonathan to help him navigate the situation. David pleaded with Jonathan not to betray him to his dad. "'Never!' Jonathan exclaimed. 'You know that if I had the slightest notion my father was planning to kill you, I would tell you at once'" (1 Samuel 20:9 NLT).

Jonathan loved David enough to deliver the hard news. We all need a friend or two in our life who will speak the hard and uncomfortable truth when we need to hear it.

If you want to experience authentic community, you need at least one person around you who will be honest with you when no one else will. They need to have the freedom to speak the truth about your treatment of people, your language, your spiritual life, your relationship with your spouse and kids, your use of finances, and many other things.

Solomon said, "Wounds from a friend can be trusted" (Proverbs 27:6). When you get a couple of friends like that, hang onto them and cherish them. They are a gift. Thank God for them.

WHAT ABOUT YOU?

Do you have at least one 2 a.m. friend—a friend you can count on to come to your aide when you need help and who will tell you the truth when you need to hear it? And what about you? Are you a 2 a.m. friend to at least one other person? If you don't have this kind of friendship, begin by diligently asking God to help you cultivate these qualities in yourself and find a friend who has these qualities as well. Then be open to God's leading and enjoy the best kind of friendship this life can give.

Today's Takeaway

"A man of many companions may come to ruin, but there is a friend who sticks closer than a brother"(Proverbs 18:24).

day
19

THE BLESSING OF VOICE AND THE VOICE OF BLESSING

I saw a human interest story on television about a woman who had severe physical and emotional struggles. Her daughter had been a major source of strength and encouragement. During the interview, this woman took the camera crew upstairs to her master bathroom. The young daughter had written her mom a note on the bathroom mirror in lipstick. The note said: *"The best gift I could give you is the gift to be able to see yourself as I see you. You are my hero."* Those words had stayed on the mirror for weeks.[1]

There is tremendous power in words. Proverbs 18:21 says, "The tongue has the power of life and death." Your words have the power to breathe life and grace and hope and love to others; they also have the power to cut and slice and poison and destroy. Encouragement is a crucial element in authentic community.

Mother Teresa once said, "Kind words can be short and easy to speak but their echoes are truly endless."

The echo of Jonathan's kind words in David's life was truly endless. First Samuel 23 finds Saul still in hot pursuit of David. David caught wind of Saul's latest plot, so he went to God for some answers. He had two questions. Will Saul come down to kill David as had been rumored, and will the citizens of Keilah surrender David to Saul? God's answers were very short and to the point: "He will" and "They will" (vv. 11, 12).

In the middle of this turmoil, Jonathan paid David a visit. Notice what Jonathan did for David. "Saul's son Jonathan went to David at Horesh and helped him find strength in God" (1 Samuel 23:16).

Six short but powerful words: Jonathan "helped him find strength in God."

We don't know exactly what Jonathan said to his good friend David, but we do know that his words were life-giving to David. They encouraged, affirmed, and inspired David to find strength in his heavenly Father.

Jesus was the master at making people feel valued and encouraged. In Luke 13 Jesus healed a woman who had been crippled for eighteen years. She was so crippled that the Bible says she was unable to stand up straight.

Later in the passage, Jesus was criticized by the synagogue ruler for healing on the Sabbath. Jesus had little patience for this kind of policy-driven religion. So he fired back, "You hypocrites! Doesn't each of you on the Sabbath untie your ox or donkey from the stall and lead it out to give it water?" (Luke 13:15).

Jesus went on to say, "Then should not this woman, a daughter of Abraham, whom Satan has kept bound for eighteen long years, be set free on the Sabbath day from what bound her?" (Luke 13:16).

Notice that this time Jesus didn't just call her "woman," as he did in verse 12; he called her "a daughter of Abraham." He didn't see her as a

Mother Teresa once said, "Kind words can be short and easy to speak but their echoes are truly endless."

crippled, old woman. He saw her as a child of the great patriarch of the Jewish people. Imagine her walking home that day. She stands up straight. She sees things she hasn't seen in years. And ringing in her ears are the words "daughter of Abraham."

In a world where people are beat up and put down, we have the unbelievable privilege of saying to people, "You matter, your life counts, God loves you, you are valuable, and the God of the universe is intimately interested in you."

There is a young man in Calgary, Canada named Tyler. Tyler's in his midtwenties and has special needs. He helps out at church by distributing the mail to the staff, and after he's done, you'll find him sitting at a desk with a notebook and pen in hand. Every single day Tyler writes a dozen or so personal notes of encouragement. His dad commented that this is Tyler's way of saying, "You were on my mind today."

The writer of Hebrews challenges us to "encourage one another daily, as long as it is called 'Today,' so that none of you may be hardened by sin's deceitfulness" (Hebrews 3:13).

We must encourage each other today, because today is all we have. We can't undo yesterday, and we don't know what tomorrow holds. But we do possess "today," so let's find someone to encourage today.

WHAT ABOUT YOU?

What would it look like for you to be excessive and over the top with your encouragement this week? Singlehandedly, you can lift someone's spirits, change the atmosphere in your office, or lighten the burden of someone in your small group. Go for it!

Today's Takeaway

Your words have the power to breathe life and grace and hope and love; they also have the power to cut and slice and poison and destroy. Choose them wisely.

day
20

SCANDALOUS GRACE

Most eighty-two-year-old women are looking to retire. But Helen and Ellen Ashe are not like most eighty-two-year-old women. Every week they joyfully cook and serve two thousand needy people in Knoxville, Tennessee. Every day they also dish out a lot of hugs, all in the name of Jesus' love.

In 1984 these twin sisters started the Love Kitchen in the basement of a church. For more than twenty-five years, they have been providing meals and clothes to those in need. They affectionately say they "strive to nourish the hungry, the homeless, the helpless, the hopeless, and the homebound." These two African-American ladies have an infectious love that ministers to anybody and everybody.

Helen said, "Our daddy may have only had a third-grade education, but he could read the King James Bible. He taught us three things:

1. There is but one race—the human race.
2. There is but one Father—the heavenly Father.
3. Never take the last piece of bread from the table—save it for someone in need."[1]

Helen and Ellen, at eighty-two, demonstrate the same kind of scandalous grace that Jesus did.

John Eldredge, author of *Wild at Heart,* once said, "Modern evangelicalism reads like an IRS 1040 form: it's true: all the data is there, but it doesn't take your breath away."[2] How sad that we have taken the love story of Scripture and turned it into mere facts and information.

Today you will hear a story that should boggle your mind, stop you in your tracks, and take your breath away. This is not one of the well-known stories about David. It takes place in 2 Samuel 9 and very well could be one of his most shining moments.

By this time David is the king of Israel and he is living the dream. There is peace and unparalleled prosperity in the land. David is soaking in the goodness of God. He was once a no-name shepherd boy, and now he is the king. And then one day, he remembers a conversation he had twenty years earlier with his good friend Jonathan.

In that conversation, Jonathan and David had made a covenant together that no matter where life led them, they would always show kindness to each other and each other's families. But Jonathan had been tragically killed in battle years earlier; and in those days, any remaining family members of a deposed king were quickly executed to put down any chance of an uprising.

David asked, "Is there anyone?" It is a question dripping with grace.

After Jonathan's death, everyone in the palace had begun to flee, fearing for their lives. A nurse picked up Jonathan's five-year-old son Mephibosheth and tried to run out of the palace. However, in the rush, she fell—and young Mephibosheth was crippled for life (2 Samuel 4:4). On that fateful day of his father's death, this boy's entire destiny changed.

One day he was running around the palace like any other five-year-old. The next day he was an orphan and a fugitive who was now crippled for life.

We know nothing of Mephibosheth for the next twenty years. While King David's power and fame soared, Mephibosheth surely lived a life of isolation and pain.

After those twenty years, one day David asked, "Is there anyone left of the house of Saul to whom I can show kindness for Jonathan's sake?" (2 Samuel 9: 1). David didn't ask, "Is there anyone deserving?" or, "Is there anyone that would make a good cabinet member?" No. David asked, "Is there anyone?" It is a question dripping with grace.

But listen to the servant's response. "Yes, there is someone, but he is a cripple." It's as if he was saying, "I doubt you would want him around. He really wouldn't fit in well. He's not really royal material."

But David would not be dissuaded. He sent for Mephibosheth.

Imagine the emotions Mephibosheth must have felt during that chariot ride to the king's palace: fear, anxiety, panic, uncertainty. He likely thought he would be killed. Maybe if he threw himself on the mercy of the king, just maybe . . . his life would be spared.

Before David could say anything, Mephibosheth fell to the floor and said, "I am your servant." But David's first words to him were again filled with grace, "Don't be afraid." He said, "You've got it all wrong. I am here to show you kindness and to restore to you the land that belonged to your grandfather Saul."

But it didn't add up. So, Mephibosheth said, "Who is your servant, that you should show such kindness to a dead dog like me?" (2 Samuel 9:8).

David's unexpected display of grace left him reeling. He was a nobody. He was crippled. He had absolutely nothing to offer.

Then came the icing on the cake. David said, "And you will always eat at my table" (2 Samuel 9:10). Just so we don't miss this outrageous display of grace, it is repeated four times in this brief passage. Mephibosheth, a crippled fugitive, was now being included in the royal family.

Do you think Mephibosheth understood grace? Every time he hobbled to the table and slipped into his seat, the tablecloth of grace covered his brokenness and welcomed him into fellowship with the family.

At the heart of authentic community is grace. We have to create a safe place where people can show up with their brokenness. And when we are filled with grace, we say, "It's not just safe here, but you are welcomed and accepted. And, just like David, we desire to lavish you with grace. Because after all, we are broken too and have been the undeserving recipients of God's scandalous grace."

WHAT ABOUT YOU?

Have you felt God's undeserved grace? Has your heart been overwhelmed and surprised, like Mephibosheth, with God's invitation to sit at his table and be a part of his family? And on the flip side, do you show this kind of grace to the outcasts of society you come across? Do you view them with the dignity God has bestowed on them? Maybe the woman in line in front of you who is fumbling to count out her food stamps? Or the homeless person on the street asking for spare change? Do you see these people as God sees them? Of such is the evidence of grace.

Today's Takeaway

At the heart of authentic community are lavish,
over-the-top expressions of grace.

☏12

part 5

Supernaturally Responding to Evil with Good

JOSEPH

Do not repay anyone evil for evil . . .

Do not be overcome by evil,

but overcome evil with good.

—Romans 12:17, 21

day

21

BEING EATEN ALIVE FROM THE INSIDE

Think of the person who has hurt you the most. Does a name come to mind? Can you see his or her face in your mind's eye? Maybe it was someone who walked out on you or abused you or gossiped about you or lied to you or stole from you or betrayed you.

What did you do with that hurt? One tendency is to "stuff" the hurt and never deal with it. Another option is to live with a seething bitterness toward the person. Dealing with life's deep hurts is not easy or painless, but God has given us crystal-clear instructions on how we are to respond. Read the following passage slowly and carefully. If you're honest, you'll have to admit that these teachings are counterintuitive to what your emotions want to do when you are hurt.

But these words are the path to freedom and joy and peace of mind:

Bless those who persecute you; bless and do not curse. Rejoice with those who rejoice; mourn with those who mourn. Live in harmony with one another. Do not be proud, but be willing to associate with people of low position. Do not be conceited.

Do not repay anyone evil for evil. Be careful to do what is right in the eyes of everyone. If it is possible, as far as it depends on you, live at peace with everyone. Do not take revenge, my dear friends, but leave room for God's wrath, for it is written: "It is mine to avenge; I will repay," says the Lord. On the contrary:

"If your enemy is hungry, feed him;

if he is thirsty, give him something to drink.

In doing this, you will heap burning coals on his head."

Do not be overcome by evil, but overcome evil with good. (Romans 12:14–21)

These words from the apostle Paul mirror what Jesus taught in Matthew 5:44: "Love your enemies and pray for those who persecute you."

We are commanded to bless those who hurt us and wound us. To "bless" someone literally means to wish someone well and to desire God's favor on their lives. Before we can ever hope to bless those who have hurt us, we must choose to forgive them. Refusing to forgive and holding onto bitterness is like drinking poison and hoping the other person gets sick. When we refuse to forgive, the person we hurt the most is us.

In *Living on the Edge,* Chip outlines a three-stage process of forgiveness.[1]

Stage 1: Forgive

By an act of the will, you make the choice to forgive. You don't need to *feel* like forgiving someone to do it. The choice is completely yours. You have had no control over what this person did to you, but you have 100 percent control over your response.

Stage 2: Forgiving

This is the process whereby your choice to forgive is ongoing and over time begins to align with your emotions. This part of the process could take months or even years. Even though you have made the decision to forgive, old emotions can still rise to the surface. And when they do, you keep going back to the choice you made, and you keep asking God to remove any residue of unforgiveness in your heart. And, with time, you pray God's blessing in that person's life.

Stage 3: Forgiven

This final stage of the process happens when your emotions align with the choice you made to forgive. Now you can authentically pray for blessing in this person's life and genuinely rejoice when they are blessed.

Just to make sure there is no room for misunderstanding, in the last few verses of Romans 12, Paul gives us a couple of very strong commands. He says in verse 17, "Do not repay anyone evil for evil." Then in verse 19 he says, "Do not take revenge." There is no escape clause or loophole. It is *never* the prerogative of a Christ-follower to take revenge. Personal retaliation is like fighting a fire with a hose filled with gas.

Evil is very powerful and can leave devastation in its wake. Perhaps you have personally experienced evil's devastating impact. It may seem hard to believe, but it really is possible, by God's grace, to forgive and love those who have hurt us. By God's grace, it is possible to be set free from bitterness and resentment. The message of God for us today is that the only thing more powerful than evil is good.

> Refusing to forgive and holding onto bitterness is like drinking poison and hoping the other person gets sick.

That's why the last verse of Romans 12 says, "Do not be overcome by evil, but overcome evil with good" (v. 21).

Over the next few days, we'll be looking at the Old Testament Bible character Joseph, whose forgiving heart is hard to comprehend. He was hurt much, but he forgave completely.

WHAT ABOUT YOU?

What name came to your mind when, in the first paragraph of this devotion, you were asked to think of the person who has hurt you the most? Have you experienced the self-damage that unforgiveness can have on your heart? Are you ready to begin the three-stage process of forgiveness? If not, lay your heart out before God and ask him to do his work in you and bring you to the point of readiness. Then take that first step and keep going. You'll discover new depths of God's grace and love like you've never known before.

Today's Takeaway
You must release, not relive your hurts. Unforgiveness is like drinking poison and hoping the other person gets sick.

WHAT WE CAN LEARN FROM BANANAS

Meet a man named Joe. He grew up in a good home where he was the youngest in a large family. At the age of seventeen, he left home. Joe had never lived away from home before—he must have been nervous, even a little scared. His first job was working for a captain in the military.

Joe was a believer, and he was serious about his faith. His boss was not a Christian but could see there was something different about Joe. Joe was reliable, trustworthy, responsible, and hardworking. Joe got one promotion after another. In fact, his boss had such confidence in him that he never worried about anything Joe was responsible for.

Now, Joe was young, handsome, and well-built. It was not long until the boss's wife began to take notice of him. She flirted with him. She dressed seductively to see if she could get a response from Joe. She looked for opportunities to be alone with him. Finally, frustrated that her subtle tactics weren't working, she came right out and asked Joe to go to bed with her.

Joe was young, single, and far away from home—and a beautiful older woman tried to seduce him. What do you think he did?

This is not a story from a steamy novel. It's actually a story straight from the pages of the Bible (Genesis 39). It is the real-life, true story of Joe-seph.

Just like Joseph experienced, evil comes at us in many ways. Sometimes it is in the form of people intentionally wounding us. Sometimes it is in the form of a seductive temptation. No matter what the form of evil, the apostle Paul gave us a strategy for overcoming. He said, "Do not be overcome by evil, but overcome evil with good" (Romans 12:21). We overcome evil by doing what is good and right. Ironic as it might seem, the antidote to evil is good.

In this story, Joseph did good by doing what was right. He was a man of absolute integrity. When Potiphar's wife grabbed Joseph's coat and tried to pull him into the bedroom, the Bible says that Joseph "left his cloak in her hand and ran out of the house" (Genesis 39:12).

Joseph did the manly thing: he ran. As we all know, there are certain things "real men" don't do. Real men don't eat quiche . . . and real mean don't willingly stay in situations where they are tempted. Joseph knew the weakness of his flesh and sinful desires, and he knew that the most coura-geous thing he could do was hightail it out of there.

I wonder if Thomas Watson, former chairman of IBM, had Joseph in mind when he said, "Nothing so conclusively proves a man's ability to lead others as what he does from day to day to lead himself."

> "Nothing so conclusively proves a man's ability to lead others as what he does from day to day to lead himself."
> —Thomas Watson

Joseph was leading himself well. He had al-ready settled his convictions. His moral com-pass was firmly in place. And when he was tempted, his outward conduct matched his in-ward conviction and character.

That's integrity, and that's how you overcome evil. The word "integrity" is the idea of wholeness, that your life is "integrated" and how you act outwardly is reflective of who you are inwardly.

Every time you go to the grocery store, you trust that the bananas you buy have integrity. All you can see is the banana peel, but you trust that behind the peel is a banana. You never wonder if you're going to get home, take off the peel, and find an orange. One hundred percent of the time, you can know that you will find a banana behind the banana peel. That is integrity.

The psalmist speaks of integrity when he says, "Blessed are they who maintain justice, who constantly do what is right" (Psalm 106:3). People with integrity "constantly do what is right."

Solomon says, "People with integrity walk safely, but those who follow crooked paths will slip and fall" (Proverbs 10:9 NLT). Notice that he doesn't say people with integrity walk easily. Sometimes it's hard to walk with integrity, and integrity comes with a price tag. Joseph found this out. He ended up in prison as a result of doing what was right. But God would ultimately vindicate and bless his integrity.

WHAT ABOUT YOU?

How is your integrity these days? Ask the Holy Spirit to shine the spotlight on any area where there is inconsistency between your inner life and outward actions. Then ask your Father to show you how to bring your actions in line with your convictions.

Today's Takeaway
The distance between your convictions
and your conduct is your integrity gap.

UNKNOWN DOESN'T EQUAL UNIMPORTANT

"From God's perspective, anonymous seasons are sacred spaces. . . . Unapplauded, but not unproductive: hidden years are the surprising birthplace of true spiritual greatness."[1]

This was certainly true of Jesus. We tend to forget that the stories about him reflect a very short time period. Of the eighty-nine chapters in the Gospels, only four give us any insight into Jesus' life before his public ministry began at age thirty. The overwhelming majority of his life was spent in total obscurity. Only for a short season was he in the public eye.

In her book *Anonymous: Jesus' Hidden Years . . . And Yours,* Alica Britt Chole writes, "Jesus was born in Bethlehem in a smelly animal pen (followed by hidden days). He was circumcised in the temple on his eighth day (followed by hidden months). Before turning two, Jesus received a visit from Eastern wise men (followed by hidden years). At the age of twelve he teaches in the temple (followed by almost two entirely hidden decades)."[2]

Even though Jesus was hidden from public view during those early years, God was still at work. He was preparing, speaking, and shaping Jesus for what was to come. God must work *in* us greatly before he can work *through* us greatly.

But waiting is hard. Obscurity can be a bitter pill to swallow. The Old Testament character Joseph knew all about obscurity. When he resisted the sexual advances of Potiphar's wife, she falsely accused him, and he ended up in prison. While in prison, God's favor was on Joseph, but he was still in prison . . . unknown, forgotten, and disconnected from family. And don't forget, he was in prison for doing the right thing.

Genesis 40 begins with the words "Some time later" (v. 1). Joseph endured days and weeks and months of being punished for something he didn't do. Then he interpreted a dream for the king's cupbearer, and Joseph told him, "When all goes well with you, remember me and show me kindness" (Genesis 40:14). But the closing verse of chapter 40 says that the cupbearer "did not remember Joseph; he forgot him" (v. 23).

But God had not forgotten Joseph. Not only would God liberate him from prison, he would exalt him to a high position of influence in the government. And even more, he would reunite Joseph with his family.

We learn a valuable lesson from Joseph's season of obscurity: we learn that one of the ways we "overcome evil with good" (Romans 12:21) is through our faithfulness. Day after day, even when he couldn't see what God was doing, Joseph was faithful to God. Even though he was the victim of unfair circumstances, he kept doing what was right and good. He kept following and trusting God even when life didn't make sense.

If you're in a time of obscurity, know that God has not forgotten you.

One great thing about prison is that it provided Joseph lots of opportunity for silence and solitude. He had the ability to face the deepest issues in his life. He had time in prison to look up through the bars and see the stars. He had time to talk to God and remember the dreams God had given him as a young man. He hung on and deepened his relationship with God.

And that's what God wants for us. If you're in a time of obscurity, know that God has not forgotten you. Hebrews 10:36 says, "For you have need of endurance so that when you have done the will of God, you may receive what was promised" (NASB). Joseph was under great stress and pressure, but he endured. He remained faithful.

WHAT ABOUT YOU?

Perhaps you are experiencing a time of obscurity. Sometimes our days of obscurity are accompanied by stress and dissatisfaction. We end up asking God to change the stuff we can't control, and we forget that God's primary commitment is to change us in the midst of the stuff we don't like.

Even though you might be hidden from the world, you are not hidden from God. Allow this anonymous season to deepen rather than discourage you. Our Father God is not care-less or cause-less with our lives. He can be trusted.

Today's Takeaway
Obscurity is the classroom of character.

ᴓ12

day
24

GETTING PAST YOUR PAST

St. Benedict, a fifth-century Christian, took complaining and bitterness very seriously. In his monasteries, he saw complaining as a serious threat to the unity and relationships of the monks living there. He said, "First and foremost, there must be no word or sign of grumbling, no manifestation of it for any reason at all."[1] The most wonderful line in *The Rule of St. Benedict* describes what happens if you complain in the monastery. "Let Father Abbot send two stout monks to explain the matter to him."[2] You complain and whine in the monastery and you get a visit from a couple of monk bouncers named Guido and Vinnie.

St. Benedict knew that grumbling and resentment and bitterness are a dangerous poison with the power to destroy us and those around us. We all know people who have allowed the poison of bitterness to run and ruin their lives. We see it easily: bitterness reveals itself through negativity, criticism, anger, and dysfunction.

One of the ways to overcome bitterness is to practice gratitude. Gratitude drains the poison out of bitterness. That's why Paul challenged us, "Give thanks in all circumstances; for this is God's will for you in Christ Jesus" (1 Thessalonians 5:18).

I have some really good news for you: gratitude is totally yours to control. No one else controls it. No one can take it away from you. And you can get better and better at it . . . but you must practice.

Joseph was the poster child for practicing gratitude in spite of life's hurts. He was almost killed by his brothers. He was sold into slavery. He was falsely accused of rape. He was forgotten in prison. If anybody had good reason to be resentful, it was Joseph.

By God's providence and plan, he eventually got out of prison and was appointed as prime minister of Egypt. Joseph also got married and had two sons. He named them Manasseh and Ephraim. In English those names may not mean much, but in Hebrew they tell a powerful story of gratitude. The word *Manasseh* means 'God has caused me to forget'. Joseph was saying, "I've put the past behind me. I'm choosing to move on and look ahead. I'm letting my brothers off the hook for what they did to me. I'm not angry over being falsely accused. I'm not resentful that I was forgotten by the cupbearer. God has allowed me to forget. I've dealt with those issues."

And then notice the name of his other son. *Ephraim* means 'fruitful'. Someone has said Manasseh's name was Amnesia and Ephraim's was Ambrosia. Joseph was not only saying that God had allowed him to forget the past, but that God had also blessed him and made him fruitful in the present. Just in the naming of his two sons, we see the gratitude and spiritual maturity of Joseph.

Gratitude is totally yours to control. No one else controls it. No one can take it away from you.

Joseph trusted in God's goodness and sovereignty. He knew that even in his bad circumstances, God had a good plan. God wanted the very best for Joseph. Even when others intended evil and hurt, Joseph knew that God was bigger and could take what was intended for evil and make it good. Joseph actively believed that God's sovereign control over all circumstances was meant for his good.

Notice Paul's observation about gratitude: "Let your roots grow down into him, and let your lives be built on him. Then your faith will grow strong in the truth you were taught, and you will overflow with thankfulness" (Colossians 2:7 NLT).

WHAT ABOUT YOU?

Who has hurt you—maybe even intentionally, intending it for evil? When you are dealing with your own anger and resentment over evil inflicted on you, you need to remember that *God meant it for good.* Isaiah 30:18 says, "The LORD longs to be gracious to you."

If you really believe that God is in control and that he longs to be gracious to you, then gratitude will roll out of your heart and off your lips. Like Joseph, you will be able to say, "God has caused me to forget" and, "God has blessed me and made me fruitful."

As you walk with Christ and your roots grow down into him, your faith will grow. And one of the most powerful signs of a life rooted in Christ is overflowing gratitude. May you have overflowing gratitude as you walk through your day today.

Today's Takeaway
Gratitude drains the poison out of bitterness.

day
25

VICTIM OR VICTOR?

Joe Stack, at the age of fifty-three, set his house on fire. Then he got in a single-engine plane and flew it into an IRS building in Austin with nearly two hundred employees, killing one man.

His rage was directed toward the "system." He believed he was the victim of unfair tax codes, unjust laws, corrupt politicians, and dishonest accountants. His disappointment turned to disillusionment which led to seething anger, which culminated in one final act of desperate revenge.

Stack left behind a suicide letter, stating, "I saw it written once that the definition of insanity is repeating the same process over and over and expecting the outcome to suddenly be different. I am finally ready to stop this insanity. Well, Mr. Big Brother IRS man, let's try something different; I'll take my pound of flesh and sleep well."[1]

How does a person get there? How does someone become so consumed by rage, controlled by hate, and willing to kill himself and others for revenge?

This story is extreme, but it demonstrates the power of anger and resentment and unforgiveness. And all of us know what it is like to feel the anger, to say, "This isn't right. It's not fair." And though we may not act on it, we are angry. And we may even secretly fantasize about revenge.

How different from the teachings of Jesus. He said, "Love your enemies, do good to them, and lend to them without expecting to get anything back" (Luke 6:35).

What would you have done if you had been Joseph? This could have been the moment for crushing revenge.

In Romans 12:14, the apostle Paul reiterated Jesus' teaching. He says, "Bless those who persecute you; bless and do not curse."

Jesus and Paul knew that that if we allow bitterness to run its course, it will destroy us. And centuries before Jesus or Paul spoke these words, Joseph lived them.

He is a real, tangible example of blessing those who hurt you. The recipients of Joseph's blessing were none other than his own brothers. These are the same brothers who had contemplated killing Joseph and then decided to sell him into slavery. Their evil actions forever changed the direction of Joseph's life.

Many years later, Joseph became the prime minister of Egypt. There was a famine in the land, and his brothers come to Egypt hoping to buy some grain. Imagine this scene: Joseph's brothers are standing in line to buy food. When their turn comes, they step up and ask for food from Joseph. Now Joseph immediately recognizes them, but they don't recognize him.

Pause for a moment. What would you have done if you had been Joseph? This could have been the moment for crushing revenge. He was no longer a helpless teenager. He was second-in-command to the Pharaoh himself. Joseph could have had his brothers executed on the spot.

At first Joseph didn't reveal his true identity. But eventually he could no longer continue this charade or control his emotions. So, he told everyone else to leave the room, except for his brothers. Then he revealed that he was their younger brother, the one they had sold into slavery. By this point, he was sobbing like a baby. "And now, do not be distressed and do not be angry with yourselves for selling me here, because it was to save lives that God sent me ahead of you" (Genesis 45:5).

Joseph did not play the victim card. He did not serve up a bowl of steaming guilt and blame. Shockingly, there was no anger or hatred or resentment in his voice or words. God had long ago removed the poison of unforgiveness. Joseph was gracious, tender, redemptive, and generous toward his brothers.

Joseph not only refused to retaliate, but he blessed his brothers. He said, "Come down to me; don't delay. You shall live in the region of Goshen and be near me—you, your children and grandchildren, your flocks and herds, and all you have. I will provide for you there, because five years of famine are still to come" (Genesis 45:9–11).

WHAT ABOUT YOU?

Are you playing the victim regarding the hurts in your life, or are you claiming victory over them by refusing to retaliate—even doing the unthinkable: choosing to *bless* them? You put the love of God on display when you show love instead of hate, kindness instead of rage, and blessing instead of bitterness. You are never more like Jesus than when you bless those who have hurt you.

Today's Takeaway
You are never more like Jesus
than when you bless those who have hurt you.

THE WAY FORWARD

As you have read this book, I hope you've been inspired by the lives of these heroes of the faith. But more than that, I hope you have personally begun to feel a shift of momentum in your own life. The critical question now is, "How do you sustain the momentum?" As we come to the end of this twenty-five day journey, I want to leave you with four concluding thoughts before you put down this devotional and get on with your life.

1. *It's not easy.* The demands of the Christian life are rigorous. They are not for the weak of heart. To live like a Christian is not to pursue the "good life"; rather, it is to pursue the "God life." Words like *surrender, obedience, trust, authenticity, sacrifice* and *forgiveness* will test our mettle and stretch us way beyond our comfort zone. But, as we saw in this devotional, it is the only life worth living.

2. *I can't do it.* I have been a Christ follower for more than forty years, and I am ashamed to tell you how much I still struggle to be obedient. As long as we live in this world, life will be a battle. But here's the

good news: Living the Christian life isn't dependent on my strength or will power. God has given me the Holy Spirit as a constant companion and guide and source of power. And 2 Peter 1:3 (NLT) says, "By his divine power, God has given us everything we need for living a godly life." So, lean on the Holy Spirit and regularly ask him to fill you.

3. *I need community.* I not only need the Holy Spirit; I need other people to help me live like a Christian. I need people who know me, love me, support me, pray for me, correct me, and show me how to live the Christian life. Don't settle for shallow, superficial relationships. Take the initiative to pursue authentic community. You won't regret it.

4. *Life is a grace-journey.* The journey has many surprises and unexpected detours. Some days the journey is easy and filled with joy. Some days the journey is incredibly hard and filled with confusion. And yes, we sin and fail and stumble along the way. But let me remind you that we have a grace-filled father who is patient and who is not as concerned with our perfection as with our progress. And he is a father who is more about relationship than rules.

So enjoy the journey, and may you experience that richness of a life that is "all in."

NOTES

Introduction

1. Chip Ingram, *Living on the Edge: Dare to Experience True Spirituality* (New York: Howard Books, 2009).

2. Ibid. xx-xxi.

Day 1: Losing Can Mean Winning

1. Marc Schulman, "Surrender," HistoryCentral.com, http://www.historycentral.com/CivilWar/Surrender

2. Chip Ingram, *Living on the Edge,* 15.

Day 2: God's Cosmic GPS

1. Ed Burnette, "Viral Video: Susan's Got Talent," ZDNet, April 4, 2009, http://www.zdnet.com/blog/burnette/viral-video-susans-got-talent/1061.

Day 3: Surrendered People Have No Rights

1. Michelle Miller, "From the Streets of Memphis to the NFL: 'The Blind Side' Tells the True Story of a Homeless Teen and the Family Who Helped Him Realize His Dreams," *CBS Evening News,* November 12, 2009, http://www.cbsnews.com/stories/2009/11/12/eveningnews/main5632913.shtml.

Day 5: God's Throne Is a Single-Seater

1. A. W. Tozer, *The Pursuit of God* (1957; repr., Camp Hill, PA: WingSpread Publishers, 2010), 30.

Day 6: Father Knows Best

1. Chip Ingram, *Living on the Edge*, 68.

Day 7: Are You Following Christ or the Crowd?

1. Adolf Hitler, *Mein Kampf,* 1924.

Day 8: When to Draw a Line in the Sand

1. "Nelson Mandela—Biography," NobelPrize.org, http://nobelprize.org/nobel_prizes/peace/laureates/1993/mandela-bio.html

Day 9: Don't Be a Jerk for Jesus

1. Chris Beard, "A New Perspective for a 'Bunch of Jerks,'" *Christian Standard*, December 9, 2010, http://christianstandard.com/2010/12/a-new-perspective-for-a-%E2%80%98bunch-of-jerks%E2%80%99/.

2. Ibid.

Day 10: Saying No Requires a Higher Yes

1. Tony Blair, *Mail on Sunday*, 2 October 1994.

Day 11: Spiritual Identity Theft

1. Chip Ingram, *Living on the Edge*, 103.

2. Ibid., 103.

Day 13: Excuse Me

1. "School Excuses from Parents," Funny2.com, http://www.funny2.com/schoolexcuses.htm.

Day 15: It's About God's Presence, Not His Presents

1. Gary Lamb, resignation letter to Revolution Church read by Greg Rohlinger, June 8, 2009. Text of the resignation letter is available at http://barryboucher.typepad.com/ministers_matter/fallen/.

Day 16: Lone Ranger Christians Need Not Apply

1. Chip Ingram, *Living on the Edge,* 166.

Day 17: You've Got a Friend

1. Robert Putnam, *Bowling Alone: The Collapse and Revival of American Community* (New York: Touchstone, 2001).

2. John Ortberg, *Everybody's Normal Till You Get to Know Them* (Grand Rapids: Zondervan, 2003), 46.

Day 20: Scandalous Grace

1. www.thelovekitchen.org/newsletter/page_6.pdf

2. Brent Curtis and John Eldredge, *The Sacred Romance: Drawing Closer to the Heart of God* (Nashville: Thomas Nelson, 1997), 45.

Day 21: Being Eaten Alive from the Inside

1. Chip Ingram, *Living on the Edge,* 225-227

Day 23: Unknown Doesn't Equal Unimportant

1. Alicia Britt Chole, *Anonymous: Jesus' Hidden Years . . . And Yours* (Nashville: Thomas Nelson, 2006), 13.

2. Ibid., 8.

Day 24: Getting Past Your Past

1. *The Rule of St. Benedict*, 34.6, available at http://christdesert.org/Detailed/904.html.

2. *The Rule of St. Benedict,* as quoted in Brennan Manning, *Ruthless Trust: The Ragamuffin's Path to God* (New York: HarperCollins, 2002), 36.

Day 25: Victim or Victor?

1. Michelle Maskaly, "Pilot Crashes into Texas Building in Apparent Anti-IRS Suicide," FoxNews.com, February 18, 2010, http://www.foxnews.com/us/2010/02/18/pilot-crashes-texas-building-apparent-anti-irs-suicide/.

WHAT'S NEXT?

More Group Studies from Chip Ingram

NEW BIO
Quench Your Thirst for Life

5 *video sessions*

Cinematic story illustrates Biblical truth in this 5-part video study that unlocks the Biblical DNA for spiritual momentum by examining the questions at the heart of true spirituality.

NEW House or Home Marriage
God's Blueprint for a Great Marriage

10 *video sessions*

The foundational building blocks of marriage are crumbling before our eyes, and Christians aren't exempt. It's time to go back to the blueprint and examine God's plan for marriages that last for a lifetime.

NEW Good to Great in God's Eyes
10 Practices Great Christians Have in Common

10 *video sessions*

If you long for spiritual breakthrough, take a closer look at ten powerful practices that will rekindle a fresh infusion of faith and take you from good to great...in God's eyes.

Balancing Life's Demands
Biblical Priorities for Busy Lives

10 *video sessions*

Busy, tired and stressed out? Learn how to put "first things first" and find peace in the midst of pressure and adversity.

Effective Parenting in a Defective World
Raising Kids that Stand Out from the Crowd

9 *video sessions*

Packed with examples and advice for raising kids, this series presents Biblical principles for parenting that still work today.

Experiencing God's Dream for Your Marriage
Practical Tools for a Thriving Marriage

12 *video sessions*

Examine God's design for marriage and the real life tools and practices that will transform it for a lifetime.

Five Lies that Ruin Relationships
Building Truth-Based Relationships

10 video sessions

Uncover five powerful lies that wreck relationships and experience the freedom of understanding how to recognize God's truth.

The Genius of Generosity
Lessons from a Secret Pact Between Friends

4 video sessions

The smartest financial move you can make is to invest in God's Kingdom. Learn His design for wise giving and generous living.

God As He Longs for You To See Him
Getting a Right View of God

10 video sessions

A deeper look at seven attributes of God's character that will change the way you think, pray and live.

Holy Ambition
Turning God-Shaped Dreams Into Reality

7 video sessions

Do you long to turn a God-inspired dream into reality? Learn how God uses everyday believers to accomplish extraordinary things.

Invisible War
The Believer's Guide to Satan, Demons & Spiritual Warfare

8 video sessions

Are you "battle ready"? Learn how to clothe yourself with God's "spiritual armor" and be confident of victory over the enemy of your soul.

Living On The Edge
Becoming a Romans 12 Christian

10 video sessions

If God exists...what does he want from us? Discover the profile of a healthy disciple and learn how to experience God's grace.

Watch previews & order at www.LivingontheEdge.org

Love, Sex & Lasting Relationships
God's Prescription to Enhance Your Love Life

10 video sessions

Do you believe in "true love"? Discover a better way to find love, stay in love, and build intimacy that lasts a lifetime.

The Miracle of Life Change
How to Change for Good

10 video sessions

Ready to make a change? Explore God's process of true transformation and learn to spot barriers that hold you back from receiving God's best.

Overcoming Emotions that Destroy
Constructive Tools for Destructive Emotions

10 video sessions

We all struggle with destructive emotions that can ruin relationships. Learn God's plan to overcome angry feelings for good.

Rebuilding Your Broken World
How God Puts Broken Lives Back Together

8 video sessions

Starting over? Learn how God can reshape your response to trials and bring healing to broken relationships and difficult circumstances.

Why I Believe
Answers to Life's Most Difficult Questions

12 video sessions

Examine the Biblical truth behind the pivotal questions at the heart of human existence and the claims of the Christian faith.

Your Divine Design
Discover, Develop and Deploy Your Spiritual Gifts

8 video sessions

How has God uniquely wired you? Discover God's purpose for spiritual gifts and how to identify your own.

Watch previews & order at www.LivingontheEdge.org